CONSPI

CONSPIRACY THEORY

The Story of an Idea

IAN DUNT & DORIAN LYNSKEY

WEIDENFELD & NICOLSON

First published in Great Britain in 2024 by Weidenfeld & Nicolson,
an imprint of The Orion Publishing Group Ltd
Carmelite House, 50 Victoria Embankment
London EC4Y 0DZ

An Hachette UK Company

1 3 5 7 9 10 8 6 4 2

A CIP catalogue record for this book is
available from the British Library.

ISBN (Mass Market Paperback) 978 1 3996 1286 9
ISBN (eBook) 978 1 3996 1287 6
ISBN (Audio) 978 1 3996 1288 3

Typeset by Input Data Services Ltd, Bridgwater, Somerset

Printed in Great Britain by Clays Ltd, Elcograf, S.p.A.

MIX
Paper | Supporting
responsible forestry
FSC
www.fsc.org FSC® C104740

www.weidenfeldandnicolson.co.uk
www.orionbooks.co.uk

Any fact becomes important when it's connected to another. The connection changes the perspective; it leads you to think that every detail of the world, every voice, every word written or spoken has more than its literal meaning, that it tells us of a Secret. The rule is simple: Suspect, only suspect.
— Umberto Eco, *Foucault's Pendulum*

INTRODUCTION
What Is a Conspiracy Theory?

Not so long ago, conspiracy theories felt almost cosy. Back in the 1990s, audiences would settle down to watch *The X-Files* on a Thursday night. Stoner friends would stick posters of UFOs to their bedroom walls. Rappers like the Wu-Tang Clan would spin thrilling webs of hidden connections and secret codes. Even long-running conspiracy theories about the assassination of John F. Kennedy were introduced to a new generation by the reassuring, all-American Kevin Costner in Oliver Stone's movie *JFK*. How could anything featuring Kevin Costner be dangerous?

Now, though, this way of thinking has metastasised into something corrosive, vicious and deadly. Donald Trump used a conspiracy theory to try and overturn an election, inspiring a mob assault on the US Capitol. Deranged internet subcultures concerned with non-existent satanic paedophile rings sparked terrorist violence in the real world. Worldwide protests against COVID-19 restrictions threatened to turn the worst public health emergency of our lifetime into something even more severe.

By the early 2020s, the fringe had colonised the mainstream. Conspiracism had become a psychological addiction, a political strategy and a booming industry. It took in the world's richest man (Elon Musk), its most successful public intellectual (Jordan B. Peterson), its most popular podcaster (Joe Rogan) and its most powerful man (Donald Trump). Leading US politicians like Marjorie Taylor Greene amplified the most outlandish far-right conspiracy theories available online and, far from being ostracised, actually advanced their careers. In the UK, front-bench politicians like Suella Braverman echoed the anti-migrant language of far-right conspiracy theories about a deliberate plan to replace native populations. Former culture secretary Nadine Dorries wrote a wild-eyed book about an alleged conspiracy inside the British government while literally serving in that government. Former prime minister Liz Truss talked about a 'deep state' trying to undermine British democracy, in a desperate attempt to justify her own extensive political failures. It felt as if the world had gone mad – as if fiction were now as powerful as reality.

More and more, we look at our political opponents and realise that our differences are no longer about opinions or even values. They are about the existence of a shared reality. We often seem to be living in different dimensions. As a result, the possibility of reasonable discussion and civil disagreement seems increasingly like the naïve dream of a bygone era. Conspiracy theories are no longer the territory of entertaining TV shows, hip hop lyrics or late-night chats in smoky student rooms. They are an existential threat to liberal democracy.

It is now terrifyingly clear that we were wrong all along to assume that conspiracy theories were the preserve of a kooky, powerless minority. At various times throughout the last few centuries, they have burst forth from the shadows to warp entire societies and justify mass murder. Conspiracism has altered the course of history for the worse, and it has the power to do so again.

It goes without saying that the origin of the term *conspiracy theory* has itself inspired a conspiracy theory. According to this version of events, the CIA invented the term in 1963 to discredit anybody who questioned the official investigation into the assassination of President Kennedy. It also goes without saying that this is abject nonsense. Although the phrase only became widespread after Kennedy's death, it had been circulating since at least 1863, and its origin had nothing to do with the CIA, which at that point did not exist.

What exactly is a conspiracy theory? The *Oxford English Dictionary* says it is 'the theory that an event or phenomenon occurs as a result of a conspiracy between interested parties', specifically 'a belief that some covert but influential agency (typically political in motivation and oppressive in intent) is responsible for an unexplained event'. The European Commission suggested a similar definition in 2020: 'the belief that certain events or situations are secretly manipulated behind the scenes by powerful forces with negative intent'.

These are not particularly helpful definitions. The reason they're not helpful is that those beliefs are sometimes well founded. During the US Iran–Contra affair in the 1980s, for instance, officials in Ronald Reagan's administration secretly facilitated illegal arms sales to Iran in order to fund anti-communist militias in Nicaragua. It was top-grade conspiracy material – powerful men in the heart of Washington breaking their own laws in order to supply weapons to religious fanatics and funnel money to murderous far-right paramilitaries. And it was entirely true. There are many other stories like this one. Paranoia is sometimes justified. There *are* powerful forces with negative intent. There *are* covert agencies. There *are* conspiracies. To get over this problem, the historian Daniel Pipes characterised a conspiracy theory as 'the fear of a non-existent conspiracy'. But how can you know straight away that a conspiracy is non-existent? Journalists and historians have to weigh the evidence, and it sometimes take decades to decisively conclude that a plot did or did not exist. The journalist David Aaronovitch therefore countered with a sturdier and far more effective definition: 'the unnecessary assumption of conspiracy when other explanations are more probable'.

This clarifies two classes of belief. There are theories about a conspiracy – hypotheses where someone might reasonably believe that a conspiracy has taken place on the basis of the available evidence. And there are conspiracy theories – hypotheses where someone cannot reasonably believe that a conspiracy has taken place on the basis of available evidence, but they do so anyway. A real conspiracy usually involves a small number of people with prior relationships pursuing a limited objective with variable success. An imagined conspiracy, however, involves a huge cast of seemingly unconnected characters, somehow capable of watertight secrecy, working towards a vastly more complicated goal with superhuman efficiency.

The scholar Michael Barkun usefully divided conspiracy theories into three broad categories. The first is the 'event conspiracy theory'. This involves a single incident – 9/11, the Kennedy assassination, the COVID-19 pandemic – that is so shocking and consequential that the official explanation just won't do. The second is the 'systemic conspiracy'. This is exponentially more ambitious. It proposes that all events such as the ones listed above are the fault of a malevolent international cabal: the communists, the Jews, the Illuminati, whoever. The cast of characters changes but the structure remains the same: good versus evil, international elites versus patriotic citizens, Us versus Them. And when systemic conspiracy theories are connected into a giant hierarchy that has been pulling the strings for centuries, perhaps under the command of evil extraterrestrials, they produce a third category: the 'superconspiracy theory'. A totalising story that encompasses everything. A kind of religion. A sinister secret history of the world.

The origin of COVID-19 is a good example of the distinction between Barkun's three categories. Currently, the most likely explanation is that the virus leapt from animals to humans in a wet market in Wuhan, China, where the pandemic began in December 2019. But the consequences – lockdowns, recessions, millions dead – were so extreme that many people found it hard to put it down to simple bad luck, so other theories naturally developed.

One theory is that the virus leaked from a lab. The most reasonable version of this hypothesis is that scientists working on coronaviruses in a laboratory in Wuhan created an exceptionally virulent strain that somehow escaped into the city, and the Chinese government covered up the accident. This is not a ridiculous idea. It has inspired serious investigation by the World Health Organization and various intelligence agencies. It is therefore a theory about a conspiracy. And that is what it will remain until it is either refuted or proved.

Another version of the lab-leak hypothesis is much more dramatic. In this telling, the virus was designed as a bioweapon, albeit an incredibly inefficient one, which either leaked or was deliberately released. This is an event conspiracy theory. And then there is the far-out idea that the virus never existed, and the entire pandemic was a hoax to wreck economies and trample on civil liberties. This is a systemic conspiracy theory of the highest order.

It is perfectly possible for somebody to believe a theory about a single conspiracy and no others. A 2013 poll found that 63 per cent of Americans believed in at least one. But conspiracy theories are extremely moreish: once you pop, you can't stop. Escalation is inherent to the conspiracist worldview. In *Suspicious Minds: Why We Believe Conspiracy Theories*, Steve Brotherton observed that Americans who believe that the government is concealing evidence of extraterrestrial life in the Nevada military base Area 51 are more likely to oppose vaccines, and Britons who think climate change is a hoax are more likely to think Princess Diana was assassinated by the royal family. Incredibly, this is true even when the theories are mutually contradictory. A study by Mike Wood and Karen Douglas found that people who believed that Diana had been murdered were more likely to believe that she was still alive.

Conspiracist thinking, then, is not a rational response to the facts but a psychological disposition. The American historian Richard Hofstadter called this 'the paranoid style': 'It is, above all, a way of seeing the world and of expressing oneself.' As Hofstadter laid out in his classic 1964 essay 'The Paranoid Style in American Politics', it is a worldview that interprets events in terms of plots and secrecy. To suspect something fishy about one dramatic event is legitimate. But to imagine a conspiracy behind every terrorist attack, assassination, plane crash, premature death, viral outbreak or natural disaster is a symptom of the paranoid style. Event theories tend to lead inexorably to systemic theories. As the influential conspiracy theorist David Icke told an audience in 2014: 'People say I see conspiracies everywhere. I don't. I see one conspiracy that takes different forms.'

Barkun wrote that all conspiracy theories are founded on three essential premises: nothing happens by accident, nothing is as it seems, and everything is connected.

What unites these three beliefs is a certain relationship to knowledge. Each premise rejects coincidences and accidents, even though we see coincidences and accidents in our own lives all the time. They deny the fundamental chaos, uncertainty and fallibility of life. In the paranoid mind, everything is concerted, organised, orchestrated, planned. Perhaps it is consoling, in a pseudo-religious way, to think that planes do not crash simply due to mechanical failure and troubled men do not just walk into schools carrying assault rifles – to believe that someone, somewhere is in charge. As the journalist Fred Kaplan wrote: 'The existence of a secret cabal means that there's some sort of order in the world; a catastrophic fluke suggests there's a vast crevice of chaos, the essence of dread.'

As the double meaning of the word 'plot' suggests, every conspiracy theory is a narrative. As we shall see, novels, films and TV shows like *The Da Vinci Code*, *The Matrix* and *The X-Files* have played a vital if inadvertent role in the popularisation of conspiracism.

Recent research points to the importance of storytelling as something innate in our brains rather than our culture. We all seek patterns and narratives in order to make sense of an immensely complex world because that is part of being human. We all delight in discovering a connection between two apparently unrelated people or events. You may have seen the popular meme from the sitcom *It's Always Sunny in Philadelphia*, in which a wild-eyed Charlie Day rants in front of a pinboard covered with documents connected by red thread. Conspiracist storytelling is like Lego, with the same satisfying childlike sense of play and completion. You can move the bricks around or introduce new ones, but they always fit together with a pleasing click. Joining the dots is what our brains want to do. But that does not make every perceived connection real or significant.

'[Two ideas] are exactly what you want in a drama: everything's connected and nothing is a coincidence,' said Dennis Kelly, the writer of Channel 4's 2013–14 conspiracy thriller *Utopia*. 'That's just not how the world works though. The world is floppy and strange and bizarre and there are lots of dead ends. The really important thing is narrative isn't real. What's so alluring about conspiracies is they're narratives.' As Hofstadter wrote: 'The paranoid mentality is far more coherent than the real world, since it leaves no room for mistakes, failures, or ambiguities.'

More specifically, conspiracy theories are stories about power – who has it, how they use it, what they want. They are an alternative explanation of politics, but one that is emotional rather than factual. Many conspiracy theories are so full of holes and hard to follow that even the people who believe them often cannot elucidate how they work. Their political purpose is therefore not really explaining what happened but identifying scapegoats. This is why today they are inseparable from populism and extremism. Wherever they arise, conspiracy theories see the world in terms of Us versus Them, the in-group versus the out-group, the people versus the elite, the native versus the immigrant. It is a form of storytelling that aims to identify and demonise the enemy.

Conspiracy theories start from reasonable instincts. It is healthy to be sceptical of power, to question orthodoxy and to want the best for your community. But these impulses become corrupted by the need for a grand narrative. They take a germ of factual truth, like a real event or group, and combine it with an emotional truth, like a sense of distrust or injustice, before building a fictitious story around it.

Counter-knowledge – the things your teachers and the media won't tell you – is an alluring thing. We all remember what it was like in school. Whatever was said in the history classroom was either boring or suspect. But the things our favourite band said about history or a friend shared in a corner of the playground were treated like nuggets of hidden truth. As Barkun wrote: 'The belief must be true because it is stigmatized.'

In adulthood, this kind of outsider information gives us a prized place in society, defined as we are by our ability to see things others cannot. It makes us the heroes of our own stories. Conspiracy theorists see themselves as agents of history rather than its impotent victims. They are heroic members of a rebel alliance of warriors for truth. It is a profoundly seductive storyline to involve yourself in: there is a vast plot that has fooled most of the world but you are the plucky detective with the wit and courage to uncover it. Conspiracy theories therefore provide all sorts of attractive propositions to the believer: a sense of order, a community of like-minded fellow truth-seekers and a starring role in events.

Conspiracy theorists deploy what appear to be the usual tools of research and argumentation. Every footnote, citation, quotation and statistic is chosen to give the hypothesis the appearance of scholarly rigour and overwhelm sceptical readers who do not have the time or expertise to verify every claim. In reality, it is a Potemkin village of academia, with all the surface provisions but none of the substance. It is only when you delve into the footnotes that you realise that conspiracy theorists mainly cite each other's work. They like to applaud quasi-experts, who have impressive credentials in an irrelevant area, and heretics, like former soldiers who hate the army or former civil servants who despise their governments. They congratulate themselves on being sceptical of mainstream sources of information, but they are amazingly credulous when it comes to any narrative that challenges the establishment view, however incoherent and self-contradicting it may be.

One essential component of serious truth-seeking is missing. It is doubt. Like scientists, historians and journalists may start with a hypothesis, but they are prepared to reject it if it is not supported by an objective analysis of multiple sources. They engage with criticism. They lay themselves open to refutation. They have considered the possibility that they might be wrong. Conspiracy theorists, however, cannot change their minds. Unable to let go of their premise, they bend the evidence around it with relentless ingenuity. The standard mantra of 'Do your own research' is therefore disingenuous, because their research never leads to them rejecting a conspiracy theory. It merely demands that someone reads their books and those of people they approve of. They say they are 'just asking questions' but they don't want to hear the answers. They are therefore pseudo-scholars writing pseudo-history. Fiction dressed as non-fiction. Parodies of reason.

Ultimately, conspiracy theories propose that there are two versions of reality: one seen yet false, one unseen yet true. 'In the world according to conspiracy theories, the obvious answer is never correct, and there is always more to things than meets the eye,' wrote Brotherton. 'Accidents are planned, democracy is a sham, all faces are masks, all flags are false.'

This detaches believers from what most of us consider reality and thrusts them into a parallel universe that the writer and activist Naomi Klein has called 'Mirror World'. Mirror World has its own rules, logic and foundational assumptions. Once you enter it, it is difficult to leave. And its population is growing fast.

This is the Origin Story of conspiracy theories: where they came from, who promoted them, how they work and what they're doing to us. We will tell the story of conspiracy theories from the days of biblical myth to the latest bout of online hysteria. We will illuminate the logic behind different kinds of conspiracy theory and the cognitive biases that underpin them. We will explore how they have fuelled purges, wars and genocides. We will ask how new technology and the failures of conventional politics and media have made them so popular in the twenty-first century. We will explain what happens when the human propensity to make sense of the world by telling stories ends up achieving the exact opposite, and why it is so dangerous. And we will show how we might halt the advance and turn it back.

The story begins 2,000 years ago, with the Book of Revelation and the ultimate scapegoat for humanity's problems.

CHAPTER ONE
The Systemic Conspiracy Theory

Conspiracist thinking can be seen as an offshoot of apocalyptic Christianity. In the Old Testament, horrific events are the work of an angry God, punishing sinners with fires, disasters and assorted plagues. But the Book of Revelation, written in the first century AD, introduced a new agent of suffering – God's antagonist. It attributed all the evil in the world to a conspiracy between Satan and his lieutenants, the Beast and the Antichrist. This was a wild and wacky new narrative for humanity, with a lurid climax involving horrific monsters, clashing armies, lakes of fire and a final judgement. Framed as secret knowledge, Revelation proposes that eternal happiness is possible only once all the wrongdoers have been exterminated. The decisive battle of Armageddon is just around the corner. It always is.

Revelation is full of code names and cryptic numbers – most famously 666 – that invite endless reinterpretation. For John of Patmos, the book's bloodthirsty author, Satan's beasts represented the Roman Empire, which really was a repressive regime. But once Rome converted to Christianity and Paradise did not arrive, readers of Revelation naturally started seeing beasts everywhere. Kings, emperors and popes were not just political opponents but ambassadors of absolute evil.

The essence of every conspiracy theory is 'Them'. Who 'They' are changes frequently – Illuminati, Freemasons, Jews, communists, the CIA, the United Nations and so on – but the fundamental structure of thinking does not. 'They' always have certain qualities. They are unfathomably evil, extremely clever, weirdly glamorous and hypercompetent. They meet in secret, and they are responsible for everything you don't like. The Antichrist and his minions were the original 'Them'. These days, the villain in every conspiracy theory is a pale imitation of Satan.

Conspiracy theories also have an apocalyptic relationship to knowledge. Apocalypse comes from the Greek word for 'revelation', or 'unveiling'. In apocalyptic texts, prophets are granted previously concealed knowledge about the way the world works because they are righteous enough to be worthy of it. Secular conspiracy theorists are the modern version of this figure. They believe they have received secret information because they are morally and intellectually superior to the slumbering herd.

Just as millenarian Christians feel compelled to spread the word about the Second Coming, systemic conspiracy theorists dedicate themselves to alerting others to the plot. This is one reason why they are hard to dissuade. A global conspiracy theory plucks the believer out of the overwhelming muddle of billions of lives and gives them a starring role in the vanguard of history. To abdicate that responsibility would be both a dereliction of duty and a return to the insignificance of ordinary life. Who would readily abandon such a compelling internal narrative and go back to sitting in front of the TV like any other normie?

It is helpful, then, to think of the paranoid style not as a species of politics but as a transformative, all-consuming pseudo-religion. 'The adoption of the conspiracy theory can hardly be avoided by those who believe that they know how to make heaven on earth,' the philosopher Karl Popper wrote. 'The only explanation for their failure to produce this heaven is the malevolence of the devil who has a vested interest in hell.' For Popper, the systemic conspiracy theory comes from abandoning God: 'His place is then filled by various powerful men and . . . sinister pressure groups, who are blamed for having planned . . . all the evils from which we suffer.'

This is one of the great dangers of conspiracy theory. Democratic politics is based on the peaceful mediation of competing interests. It relies on the idea that we are all willing to compromise and accept partial victories. But conspiracy theories are grounded in a battle between darkness and light, in which conciliation is tantamount to surrender. 'Since what is at stake is always a conflict between absolute good and absolute evil,' wrote Richard Hofstadter, 'the quality needed is not a willingness to compromise but the will to fight things out to the finish. Nothing but complete victory will do.'

Daniel Pipes traced the two main strands of conspiracist mythology back almost 1,000 years to the Crusades. The first of these was anti-Jewish paranoia. Jews were seen, for the first time, as foreign agents – in league with Islam, sabotaging Europe from within. They were accused of crimes such as poisoning water sources and using the blood of murdered Christian children in their rituals: known as the blood libel. One particularly cruel aspect of early antisemitism was the idea that Jews were so mistreated they would inevitably seek revenge. The spectre of the vengeful Jew enabled their per-secutors to imagine themselves as their future victims. Jews were punished for power they did not possess and crimes they had not committed.

The second strand was secret societies. In 1119, the French knight Hugues de Payens established an order of warrior-monks to protect pilgrims from bandits on the way to the Holy Land. They headquartered themselves in Jerusalem's Temple Mount and called themselves the Poor Fellow-Soldiers of Christ and of the Temple of Solomon – also known by the rather snappier title of the Knights Templar. Initially consisting of just nine knights, they gradually secured papal support and a flood of donations from the European aristocracy. While the Templars included a formidable fighting unit, most of their members were civilians who operated an early form of banking, guarding the assets of pilgrims and crusaders while they were away. As a result, they became integral to the life of Christendom. They were arguably the world's first multinational corporation.

The fate of the Templars was bound up with the Crusades. Muslim armies seized Jerusalem in 1244 and took complete control of the Holy Land in 1303. No longer militarily important, the Templars were now resented for their financial power and international connections. In 1307, King Philip IV of France had the Templar Grand Master, Jacques de Molay, arrested along with scores of his members. Philip convinced Pope Clement V to order the detention of Templars across Europe, the confiscation of their assets and the dissolution of the order. Leading Templars, including de Molay, were tortured into making false confessions of fraud and blasphemy and burned at the stake. As we shall see, the apparent crushing of the Templars gave rise to centuries of rumours that they were still operating through proxy secret societies. Whether satirised by Umberto Eco in 1988's *Foucault's Pendulum* or breathlessly popularised by Dan Brown in 2003's *The Da Vinci Code*, theories about the Templars are relatively harmless, except when they merge with theories about Freemasons, Illuminati and Jews.

Over the next few centuries, these twin paranoias about Jews and secret societies would often emerge in times of crisis and trauma. When the Black Death swept through Europe in the middle of the fourteenth century, killing around half the population, medical science was centuries away from being able to identify its cause. Many fearful Christians naturally attributed it to the wrath of God, but others looked for terrestrial malefactors. One eccentric theory blamed an international conspiracy headquartered in Spain. A widespread rumour that Jews were poisoning the wells led to gruesome pogroms that wiped out many Jewish communities.

Another popular scapegoat was entirely illusory: the witch. Conspiracy theories always exploit new forms of communication. The witch-hunting German priest Heinrich Kramer's 1486 work *Malleus Maleficarum (Hammer of Witches)* was an early beneficiary of the invention of the printing press and became one of history's most lethally influential books. For two centuries it was Europe's second bestselling book after the Bible. The villains in conspiracy theories adore secret societies, nocturnal meetings, initiation rituals and the infiltration of communities behind a mask of innocence. Witches ticked all those boxes. The witch craze Kramer ignited was a conspiracy theory that lasted more than 300 years and killed tens of thousands of women.

'Witches' were usually accused of making their neighbours' children sick or causing their crops to fail, but the show trials in Salem, Massachusetts, in 1692 were more ambitious. One defendant was forced to confess that Satan's plan was to abolish Christianity in Salem and then spread its evil ideas throughout America. In this satanic new society, 'all persones should be equall' – the worst imaginable outcome for a hierarchical society. Usually it was foreigners, social outsiders or followers of other religions who were accused of evil plots. But the hysteria of Salem targeted ordinary members of the community. The enemy within could be anybody.

The Black Death pogroms and the witch hunts were a primordial form of conspiracist thinking, but they were qualitatively different to what we experience today. They operated in a social and psychological context that was fundamentally distinct from ours, when religion rather than reason was thought to offer answers for events in the material world.

Modern conspiracy theories only really came into existence once reason was accepted as the appropriate way of looking at the world. They are the dark mirror to the Enlightenment.

If the conspiracy theory as we know it began anywhere, it was in Bavaria on 1 May 1776, with a 28-year-old law professor called Adam Weishaupt. Weishaupt was a passionate Enlightenment intellectual who believed that the Jesuit authorities were suppressing knowledge and stifling humanity's potential. He decided to form a group of outstanding individuals dedicated to promoting freedom, equality and rationalism. The group was called the Illuminati, which to him represented 'enlightening the understanding by the sun of reason, which will dispel the clouds of superstition and of prejudice'. He dreamt of a meritocratic brotherhood of rationality that transcended the divisions of class, religion and national borders. He could never have guessed that he had chosen a name that would inspire political nightmares for centuries to come.

Weishaupt's justified fear of Jesuit surveillance and

infiltration led him to adopt clandestine methods that made the Illuminati appear distinctly shady: codes, rituals, covert meetings. Weishaupt's code name was Brother Spartacus. Political paranoiacs often mimic their enemies – they fight secrecy with secrecy and plots with plots. The Illuminati became a kind of cult, which separated its members from friends and family in the name of total obedience. After a while, some Illuminati infiltrated a much older secret society and recruited many of its members to the cause. That group was the Freemasons – another source of perennial suspicion and crazed fantasies. They were a guild of English stonemasons, founded in the late fourteenth century, who had evolved into an international fraternity of Enlightenment free-thinkers. Open to all religions, they saw God as an architect rather than an autocrat – their task was to understand his grand design rather than follow his rules. Inevitably, the Vatican denounced Masonry for the first time in 1737.

To enhance their mystique, the Freemasons cooked up a dubious history in which they were the custodians of ancient secrets passed down from the Egyptians through heretical sects: the Gnostics, the Cathars, the Knights Templar, the Rosicrucians. They had no idea that this fanciful genealogy would one day be used against them. Their elaborate initiation rituals, secret handshakes, code names and symbology aroused fascination and suspicion. In reality, most Freemasons were boring, prosperous establishment figures, but their enemies spread the theory that the leaders were plotting a revolution, a conspiracy so secret that not even ordinary members realised it: the 'double doctrine'.

The Illuminati was just one of many Mason-inspired secret societies in eighteenth-century Europe. The continent was awash with men who liked dressing up and acting as though they were more important than they really were. Some conspiracy theorists even thought that the Illuminati had forged a secret alliance with the Freemasons at the 1782 Congress of Wilhelmsbad. Weishaupt imitated the Masons' use of mysticism and mythology but saw the Illuminati as far superior. His secret society was going to do nothing less than liberate humankind from tyranny and superstition.

This plan did not work out. Soon the Bavarian government took against the Illuminati. In 1785, it banned all secret societies and Weishaupt fled Bavaria. By 1787, the group was completely defunct. And that's it. That's the story of the Illuminati – the actual objectively real group that existed in history, rather than the one that people made up elaborate claptrap about afterwards. At its peak, it had at most 2,500 members, many of whom violently disagreed with one another. They were young and powerless and they accomplished nothing. There was no obvious reason to talk about the Illuminati ever again. But in 1789, something occurred that was so radically new it rendered conventional explanations of political change inadequate.

This was the French Revolution. Nothing like it had ever happened before. Its delighted supporters thought the future had arrived. 'Old things seemed passing away, and nothing was dreamt of but the regeneration of the human race,' wrote the English poet Robert Southey.

Those who saw the revolution as a hellish development, especially once it mutated into the Jacobins' murderous Reign of Terror, needed somebody to blame. Secret societies made a very attractive target. They were often supporters of the Enlightenment principles that had birthed the revolution, they behaved suspiciously and they were international. Indeed, several key revolutionaries, like Marquis de Lafayette and

Voltaire, were genuine Freemasons, and a few minor figures were bona fide former Illuminati. But in reality, the revolutionaries were often just as paranoid and hostile towards secret societies as their opponents. The Jacobins actually outlawed Freemasonry in 1791.

That, however, did nothing to dispel the clamour for a compelling storyline to explain the revolution. A number of pamphlets that circulated in Europe during the 1790s identified the Illuminati as the driving force. In 1797, these pamphlets were expanded into two popular books: *Memoirs Illustrating the History of Jacobinism*, by the exiled French Jesuit priest Augustin Barruel; and the more verbose *Proofs of a Conspiracy Against all the Religions and Governments of Europe, Carried on in the Secret Meetings of Freemasons, Illuminati, and Reading Societies, Collected from Good Authorities*, by John Robison, a Scottish physicist and inventor.

Both authors used extensive research into the real activities of the Illuminati as the foundation for wild claims that the revolution was the result of a multi-century conspiracy between the Illuminati and the Freemasons. Robison argued that it was part of 'one great and wicked project fermenting and working all over Europe', whose 'real intention was to abolish all religion, overturn every government, and make the world a general plunder and a wreck'. Barruel likewise claimed that the events in France had been 'foreseen, contemplated, contrived, resolved upon, decreed' as a prelude to 'that general Revolution which is to overthrow all thrones, all altars, annihilate all property, efface all law, and end by dissolving all society'. Scary stuff. This was the birth of the one-big-plot systemic conspiracy theory: a skeleton key that could unlock all of history's mysteries and expose its villainous manipulators.

Obnoxiously bossy though he may have been, the earnest, idealistic Weishaupt now looks like an unlikely candidate for the role of 'human devil', as Robison claimed, but these frenzied political anxieties would have made perfect sense at the time. In the 1790s, as France's experiment in liberal democracy descended into the Terror, conservatives associated liberty and equality with the guillotine. Barruel and Robison's evidence was tenuous and their conclusions fantastical, but both books sold tremendously well. The philosophical forefather of conservatism, Edmund Burke, praised Barruel's scholarship: 'The whole of the wonderful narrative is supported by documents and proofs with the most juridical regularity and exactness.'

In the infant republic of the United States of America, these books were devoured by members of Alexander Hamilton's Federalist Party, who were sceptical of democracy and feared that the anti-Federalists were plotting their own Reign of Terror. Hamilton suggested that a foreign power might use 'cabal, intrigue, and corruption' to install their puppet as president.

In 1798, the pastor Jedediah Morse delivered three influential sermons based on Robison's book that warned of an Illuminati-led international conspiracy to bring godless violence to America by infiltrating its institutions. Next, he warned, the Illuminati would lead a Haitian invasion of the US, recruiting slaves as they marched through the South. Morse had previously supported the French Revolution and needed an excuse for why it had gone awry. It turned out he had not been wrong after all, but hoodwinked by an evil elite.

His sermons caught the attention of former president George Washington, who wrote, in a rare lapse of judgement, that he was completely 'satisfied' that 'the doctrine of the Illuminati and the principles of Jacobinism' had spread to the US. However, he made sure to exclude the Freemasons from the plot, on the basis that he was a Freemason himself. Washington's Federalist successor as president, John Adams, exploited this hysteria to introduce a series of draconian acts aimed at 'aliens' and political opponents. The more level-headed Thomas Jefferson, who became the first Democratic-Republican president in 1801, considered Weishaupt nothing more than an 'enthusiastic philanthropist' and dismissed Barruel's book as the ravings of a madman. The defeated Federalists predictably accused him of belonging to the Illuminati himself, using his strong ties to France against him. Paranoia about un-American imposters has been in the nation's bloodstream ever since.

Once the paranoid style had taken root in America, it found new targets. In 1826, a former Freemason in New York State, William Morgan, was kidnapped by Masons while writing an exposé of the order and never seen again. He was most likely murdered. Fuelled by opposition to future president Andrew Jackson, who was a Mason, the focus of the one-big-plot conspiracy theory shifted from the ghost of the Illuminati to the genuinely active and influential Freemasons.

Most conspiracy theories start with some objective truths. The Masons *were* a privileged elite fraternity who occupied a disproportionate number of high offices. Some of its members *had* abducted William Morgan. But the short-lived Anti-Masonic Party went much further. It ran on the claim that the Masons had established a treasonous shadow government that pulled Washington DC's strings. An 1829 book, *Light on Masonry*, described the group as 'an engine of Satan . . . dark, unfruitful, selfish, demoralizing, blasphemous, murderous, anti-republican and anti-Christian'. Hyperbole is essential to the paranoid style. The conspiracy must always be unprecedented in its scale and malevolence.

It was the Catholics' turn next. A Jesuit, Augustin Barruel, had popularised fear of the Illuminati; now the Jesuits themselves were the alleged plotters. In 1835, Samuel Morse, son of Jedediah and inventor of Morse code, and Lyman Beecher, the preacher father of *Uncle Tom's Cabin* author Harriet Beecher Stowe, both published books alleging that Jesuits working on behalf of European kings were undermining the US from within. Morse's had the exciting title *Foreign Conspiracy Against the Liberties of the United States*, while Stowe claimed that puppet politicians were flooding the country with Catholic European immigrants in order to transform the electorate and sell the US 'into an everlasting bondage' – an early version of the twenty-first-century Great Replacement Theory, which we'll come to later.

Some anti-Catholic nativists formed the Know Nothing movement, which fought secrecy with secrecy: when asked about the group, they were meant to say: 'I know nothing.' New Protestant movements also inspired suspicion. Conspiracy theories about the secret intentions of Mormons, Shakers and Jehovah's Witnesses led to prejudice and violence.

On the left, capitalism itself was a conspiracy. The populist argument that small but powerful elites are thwarting the hopes of the people is not a conspiracy theory in itself, but it can be a gateway. In 1892, the founding platform of the People's Party warned of a 'vast conspiracy against mankind' that 'forebodes terrible social convulsions, the destruction of civilization, or the establishment of an absolute despotism'. Its author was the eccentric Minnesota politician Ignatius Donnelly, who had previously written bestselling books about the lost city of Atlantis and the theory that Shakespeare's plays had actually been written by Francis Bacon. The party's presidential candidate in the 1896 and 1900 elections, William Jennings Bryan, went on to become the country's leading creationist, denying the theory of evolution.

Conspiracy theories, then, were a constant feature of American life. They were blossoming all over the place – among Catholics and Protestants, right and left, churchgoers and free-thinkers. In his 2013 book *The United States of Paranoia*, Jesse Walker criticised Richard Hofstadter for claiming that the paranoid style was a minority phenomenon. In fact, he countered, the paranoid style *is* American politics. Nineteenth-century elites had their own conspiracy theories about the People's Party, striking workers, liberated slaves and even homeless men. At times it could seem as if everybody was accusing everybody else of perpetuating a conspiracy – a mania spoofed by Mark Twain in an unfinished 1890s novel called *Tom Sawyer's Conspiracy*.

One form of paranoia that was relatively quiet at that time was antisemitism. Neither Robison nor Barruel mentioned Jews in their anti-Illuminati diatribes. In fact, Barruel refused to publish a letter from a reader who blamed the Jews for the Illuminati in case it sparked pogroms. But he was privately convinced by the theory and reportedly wrote an unpublished manuscript about the connection between Jews and Freemasons, pulling together the two strands of Europe's paranoid style into a new theory of an invisible empire. The historian Norman Cohn claimed: 'In its modern form the myth of the Jewish world conspiracy can be traced back to . . . the Abbé Barruel.'

Exactly 100 years after Barruel published his Illuminati book, an event took place that inspired the most successful antisemitic conspiracy theory of all. 'There exists a subterranean world where pathological fantasies disguised as ideas are churned out by crooks and half-educated fanatics for the benefit of the ignorant and superstitious,' wrote Cohn. 'There are times when this underworld emerges from the depths and suddenly fascinates, captures and dominates multitudes of usually sane and responsible people, who thereupon take leave of sanity and responsibility. And it occasionally happens that this underworld becomes a political power and changes the course of history.' This is precisely what happened in the early twentieth century with the *Protocols of the Elders of Zion*.

In August 1897, the Austro-Hungarian Jewish journalist Theodor Herzl was feeling optimistic. The previous year, he had invented Zionism, a form of nationalism that called for a Jewish homeland as a refuge from what he saw as Europe's incurable antisemitism. He had been partly galvanised by the Dreyfus affair, a genuine military conspiracy against Jewish captain Alfred Dreyfus that had deployed the utterly fake conspiracy theory that Jews were trying to undermine France. As the historian Hannah Arendt noted, Jews, Jesuits and Freemasons all defended themselves 'by hurling at the other charges of conspiring to world domination'.

Herzl had managed to persuade 208 delegates and 26 journalists to attend the First Zionist Congress in Basel, Switzerland. Like Weishaupt, Herzl was an idealist with a modest following. The Zionist movement was tiny and powerless – it was shunned by Europe's Jewish financial and political elites until the mid-twentieth century. But unlike Weishaupt, there was nothing clandestine about his methods. On the contrary, Herzl wanted as much publicity for his fledgling movement as possible. The Basel Program clearly spelled out the Zionists' goal of a Jewish home in Palestine.

In 1903, however, a text emerged that purported to contain the minutes of secret meetings in Basel in which the Zionists revealed their true intentions. It was called the *Protocols of the Elders of Zion*. The document was first officially published, in abridged form, in a Russian newspaper run by the ultra-nationalist Black Hundreds, although it had already been circulating in underground pamphlets for a while. In 1905, the mystic writer Sergei Nilus included the full text in the second edition of his book *The Great Within the Small*, in a chapter called 'The Antichrist Considered as an Imminent Political Possibility'. He billed it as 'a manuscript that exposed with unusual perfection and clarity the course and development of the secret Jewish Freemasonic conspiracy, which would bring this wicked world to its inevitable end'.

If you are familiar with the more old-fashioned James Bond and superhero movies, then you will know the tendency of villains to explain their evil plans with great pride and relish. The *Protocols* reads like that: a manifesto for preposterous moustache-twirling perfidy. In the book, the Zionists lay out their dystopian plan to foment wars, revolutions, recessions and so on, until the world is so weak and chaotic that they can easily take it over and impose a form of tyranny that anticipates totalitarianism. 'The Gentiles are a flock of sheep,' says the leading plotter, 'and we Jews are the wolves.'

The plot is far too large to be ideologically coherent. Somehow the Elders are responsible for communism, anarchism, liberalism, republicanism, Darwinism, democracy *and* monopoly capitalism, all at the same time – in short, the entire modern world. They control the levers of labour, finance, law, science and the media.

But these apparent contradictions were exactly what made it a bulletproof 'prophecy'. If the goal of the Elders was chaos, then every war, every assassination, every famine, every economic crisis could be read as confirmation. The incoherence broadened the *Protocols'* appeal rather than limited it. So too did its absence of specific names, dates and places, leaving plenty of room for interpretation. It was not a detailed plot that could be investigated and potentially disproved, but the *template* for a plot. Notably, the book does not contain classic antisemitic tropes from the pre-Enlightenment period, such as blood libel or the betrayal of Jesus. Nor does it use Nazi-style pseudo-scientific racism. It is a distinct form of antisemitism, based on a global conspiracy theory. In this telling, the Jews are the real Illuminati.

The *Protocols'* readership was confined to Russian antisemites until the First World War and the Russian Revolution. Like the French Revolution, these were violent, earth-shaking events that required some kind of explanation. The now conventional view, that Europe sleepwalked into an unnecessary war for several complicated reasons, was not satisfactory to many people. How could it be? It was simultaneously too pedestrian and too petrifying. It suggested that millions of lives could be lost without a plan or even intention, but simply through the tragic mishaps of otherwise rational actors. It removed all sense of order and agency from the world and replaced it with a story of forced errors and unintended consequences.

In 1917, White Russian monarchists argued that the Russian Revolution confirmed the truth of the *Protocols*. They brought the text to Western Europe in an attempt to discredit Lenin's Bolshevik regime as a Jewish–Masonic conspiracy. Lenin wasn't Jewish, but many prominent revolutionaries were, including Leon Trotsky, Grigory Zinoviev and Lev Kamenev. Some German editions claimed that the speaker in the

Protocols was Theodor Herzl himself. In 1920, the *Protocols* was translated into Polish, French and English, as *The Jewish Peril*.

The early twentieth century was rife with real conspiracies. Anarchists had assassinated figures as important as US President William McKinley, King Umberto I of Italy and President Sadi Carnot of France, prompting state surveillance and subterfuge. In G. K. Chesterton's 1908 novel *The Man Who Was Thursday*, one of the great satires of paranoia, an apparent anarchist cabal turns out to consist entirely of undercover police officers. In John Buchan's bestselling 1915 thriller *The Thirty-Nine Steps*, anarchists team up with Jewish bankers to start the First World War. Professor Moriarty in the Sherlock Holmes stories is another evil mastermind with almost supernatural reach: 'The greatest schemer of all time, the organizer of every devilry, the controlling brain of the underworld.'

So while the British press accepted that the *Protocols* was antisemitic, and might not be genuine, it still insisted that there might just be something in it. *The Times* called for an urgent inquiry into the origins of the *Protocols* in the name of stifling antisemitism: 'The average man thinks that there is something very fundamentally wrong with the world he lives in. He will easily grasp at a plausible "working hypothesis".' But by taking the book seriously, the newspaper legitimised it and caused sales to soar. In the US, the automobile magnate Henry Ford serialised the *Protocols* in his newspaper, the *Dearborn Independent*, and compiled these articles into a book, *The International Jew: The World's Foremost Problem*. 'They fit with what is going on,' he said vaguely.

The mystery of the *Protocols* did not take long to solve. In August 1921, *Times* reporter Philip Graves discovered that the plot that seemed stranger than fiction was indeed fiction. The document had been substantially stolen from earlier works. Maurice Joly's 1864 satire *A Dialogue Between Machiavelli and Montesquieu* features Machiavelli, representing the French emperor Napoleon III, describing his plan for world conquest. Hermann Goedsche, a German antisemite, adapted those passages in his 1868 novel *Biarritz* to describe a conspiracy of rabbis who meet with the Devil at midnight in the Jewish cemetery in Prague. Goedsche's most damning monologues were compiled into a pamphlet, *The Rabbi's Speech*, which circulated in Russia during the late nineteenth century. Historians disagree about whether the *Protocols* was ultimately assembled in Paris on the orders of the Russian secret police, or in Russia itself by freelance cranks, but it was undoubtedly an antisemitic hoax built on plagiarism.

Graves's revelation discredited the *Protocols* in respectable circles – Henry Ford was eventually forced to apologise – but dedicated antisemites found the book far too useful to cast aside. In 1920, a series of articles about the *Protocols* and the 'world conspiracy' appeared in the British newspaper the *Morning Post* and were published in book form as *The Cause of World Unrest*. The anonymous author was an upper-class British fascist, Nesta Webster. Convinced that the Russian Revolution must be connected to the French Revolution, she published several books about secret societies and plots for world domination involving Jews, communists, Freemasons and – the group she almost singlehandedly revived interest in among the far right – the Illuminati. One of her enthusiastic readers was Winston Churchill, who wrote an article distinguishing 'good Jews' (Zionists) from 'bad Jews' (Bolsheviks). He praised Webster for identifying a 'world-wide conspiracy for the overthrow of civilisation', which had been under way 'from the days of Spartacus-Weishaupt to the days of

Karl Marx'. Not his finest hour. Gerald Winrod, a Baptist preacher and Nazi sympathiser, imported Webster's Illuminati obsession to the US with his 1935 pamphlet *Adam Weishaupt: A Human Devil*, which concluded: 'The real conspirators behind the Illuminati were Jews.' The dots had been well and truly joined.

After reading one of Webster's books, the French writer Hilaire Belloc complained to a friend about the conspiracist mindset: 'There is a type of unstable mind which cannot rest without morbid imaginings, and the conception of a single cause simplifies thought. With this good woman it is the Jews, with some people it is the Jesuits, with others Freemasons and so on. The world is more complex than that.' The more groups that were merged into the one-big-plot theory, the more absurd it should have seemed – how could so many people around the world keep the secret? But instead the combination expanded its audience.

In Germany, the *Protocols* went through 33 editions between 1920 and 1933 and was directly implicated in the assassination of Walter Rathenau, the Jewish foreign minister. For anti-semites, it did not matter if the text itself was a forgery. 'I believe in the inner, but not the factual, truth of the *Protocols*,' the leading Nazi Joseph Goebbels wrote in 1924, anticipating arguments that would be made by conspiracy theorists for decades to come. If it *felt* true, then it could not be disproven by facts and evidence.

Adolf Hitler referenced the *Protocols* in *Mein Kampf*. With classic conspiracist logic, he argued that efforts to debunk the text actually proved that it was genuine: 'With groans and moans, the *Frankfurter Zeitung* repeats again and again that these are forgeries. This alone is evidence in favour of their authenticity . . . The Jewish peril will be stamped out the moment the general public come into possession of that book and understand it.' Norman Cohn dubbed the *Protocols* a 'warrant for genocide', but it wasn't the text that turned Hitler into an antisemite – it conveniently supported the racist conclusions he had already reached. Hitler's assessment typifies the conspiracist gambit of making refutation impossible. If the conspiracy is believed to be true, then all attempts to demonstrate its falsity are in fact proof of its legitimacy.

The *Protocols* is a rare example of a conspiracy theory that has been definitively proven false. Yet to this day, more than a century after it was shown to be a hoax, it is still held up by some as an authentic text. It has featured in the books of David Icke, the teachings of the Nation of Islam, the case of the Boston Marathon bomber Tamerlan Tsarnaev and the founding charter of Hamas: '[The Zionists'] scheme has been laid out in the *Protocols of [the] Elders of Zion* and their present conduct is the best proof of what is said there.' It has been invoked by President Nasser of Egypt, Colonel Muammar al-Gaddafi of Libya and the governments of Saudi Arabia and Iran. Its long life shows that you cannot quash a conspiracy theory with facts if enough people find it politically and psychologically vital. Their need to believe and exploit it is just too strong.

The *Protocols* and the myth of the Illuminati are two versions of the same story. This history means that all systemic conspiracy theories resemble antisemitism to some degree. The popular image of the octopus strangling the globe in its tentacles, for example, had been used to represent various empires and corporations before it became a feature of Nazi propaganda against the Jews.

Nesta Webster and David Icke both insisted that the *Protocols* was actually the Illuminati's masterplan. It just so happened that *some* Jews – the Bolsheviks for Webster, 'Rothschild Zionism' for Icke – were involved. Accused of antisemitism, Icke equivocated: 'I am not saying the *Protocols* are genuine or not genuine . . . only that they tell the detailed story of the last hundred years before it happened.' When the American UFO enthusiast Milton William Cooper reprinted the *Protocols* in his influential 1991 conspiracist book *Behold a Pale Horse*, he added a disclaimer: 'Any reference to "Jews" should be replaced with the word "Illuminati".' The authors of *Holy Blood, Holy Grail*, the 1981 pseudo-history book that inspired *The Da Vinci Code*, also maintained that the *Protocols* was 'authentic' but that it had actually originated in some Masonic secret society. As Umberto Eco wrote: 'The forgery poisoned public life wherever it appeared; it was "self-generating; a blueprint that migrated from one conspiracy to another".'

Both the Illuminati and the *Protocols* present a theory of everything – the answer to all questions about history or politics. 'The distinguishing thing about the paranoid style,' wrote Richard Hofstadter, 'is not that its exponents see conspiracies or plots here and there in history, but that they regard a "vast" or "gigantic" conspiracy as *the motive force* in historical events. History *is* a conspiracy, set in motion by demonic forces of almost transcendent power, and what is felt to be needed to defeat it is not the usual methods of political give-and-take, but an all-out crusade.'

In the face of such a conspiracy, any countermeasure, up to and including genocide, is justified. The stakes are Armageddon-high and time is always desperately short. Norman Cohn argued that the one-big-plot theory remained much

the same regardless of the identity of the alleged conspirators: 'Again and again, one comes across the same weird,
apocalyptic atmosphere, hints of some gigantic final battle
in which the demonic hosts will be eliminated, the world
released from the strangling octopus, a new age brought
to birth.'

Just as followers of the sixteenth-century astrologer Nos-
tradamus endlessly reframed his prophecies in topical ways,
new editions of the *Protocols* folded the latest dire developments, from the Great Depression to 9/11, into the Elders'
plot. In the world of the giant, world-explaining conspiracy
theory, every catastrophe is merely further evidence of its
validity. Nothing that happens, anywhere in the world, is
outside of its explanatory embrace.

Similarly, stories about the Illuminati are still with us.
'The shadow of the defunct order became a specter which
took on a terrible reality for weak minds,' observed René Le
Forestier in a 1914 history of the Illuminati. Many American
fascists during the 1930s incorporated them into an imagined
conspiracy of Jews and communists, and even claimed that
Weishaupt had invented Marxism. The rabidly anti-communist John Birch Society reprinted Robison and Barruel's
books in the 1960s. Could the socialists' choice of 1 May as
International Workers' Day, they asked, be unrelated to the
date Weishaupt founded the Illuminati? Surely not. (It was.)
The Illuminati have even appeared, less earnestly, on records
by Madonna and Tupac Shakur. Jay-Z was accused of being
Illuminati so often that he joked in a song that he had been
misheard: he had said he was 'amazing', not a Mason. In his
feverish 1991 book *The New World Order*, the US evangelist
and former presidential candidate Pat Robertson implicated
the Illuminati and the Freemasons in a plot to establish a

totalitarian one-world government. And who was pulling their strings? Who was the man behind the man, controlling events? It could only be Satan himself.

In a 1938 book about the *Protocols*, the historian John Gwyer astutely observed that it was not just about antisemitism but an example of a way of thinking that he called 'the Hidden Hand'. He identified 'that unfortunate crew who can see a plot in anything. They can no longer open their newspapers, or read a book, or go to the cinema without observing the Hidden Hand at work, either involving them in subtle propaganda, or attempting to make them pawns in an elaborate scheme of sabotage.'

Decades before the rise of serious scholarship about conspiracy theories, Gwyer nailed their perverse appeal. Sufferers from paranoia, in the medical sense, are miserable and scared. It should, of course, be similarly terrifying to believe that the average person is a brainwashed pawn of malevolent schemers with limitless resources and ruthless cunning. But the paranoid style, Gwyer noted, is weirdly consoling: 'It saves so much thinking to think like this, to survey the world and know that all its disorders are due to the malignity of a single group of mysterious plotters.' Only remove the plotters and all will be well. What was once complex becomes simple again: a return to intellectual infancy.

All systemic conspiracy theories are global, moving towards a one-world government. Ever since the Knights Templar, 'globalist' organisations or groups have been objects of paranoia. The international nature of Judaism, Catholicism, Freemasonry, communism and banking disturbed nativists, who saw them as networks of foreign influence with no loyalty to any nation. Hatred of banking tends to single out the Rothschild dynasty, partly because they founded the first truly successful international bank, and partly because they are Jewish.

During the post-war decades, with antisemitism temporarily in remission, conspiracy theorists seized on any group that sought to foster international cooperation: the Council on Foreign Relations, the Trilateral Commission, the Bilderberg group. Today, they fret about such bodies as the World Economic Foundation, the European Union and George Soros's Open Society Foundations secretly plotting to enslave humanity. In one form or another, they are still talking about the Illuminati and the Elders of Zion.

CHAPTER TWO
The Paranoid State

At 9.03 p.m. on 27 February 1933, a Berlin theology student called Hans Flöter was walking home past the Reichstag, the home of Germany's parliament, when he heard the sound of breaking glass. He alerted a patrolling police officer, who saw the glow of flames inside the building and informed the fire brigade.

It is fair to say that things in Germany were already pretty tense before the fire. Adolf Hitler had just been appointed chancellor and Germans were waiting to discover how extreme the new Nazi regime would be. Hitler rushed to the scene of the blaze with his top official, Joseph Goebbels. He was met by the Reichstag president, Hermann Göring, who told him: 'Without a doubt this is the work of the communists.' A suspect had already been arrested, panting and sweating inside the Reichstag's debating chamber: 24-year-old Marinus van der Lubbe, until recently a member of the Dutch Communist Party.

Hitler had so far been at least theoretically constrained by his partners in a coalition government. Now he used the fire to his advantage. The next day, he persuaded President Hindenburg to sign the Reichstag Fire Decree, suspending civil liberties. In March, he pushed the Law to Remedy the

Distress of People and Reich through a shaken parliament, giving himself the power to single-handedly make and enforce laws without parliamentary approval. The Reichstag fire thus led directly to the establishment of the Nazi dictatorship.

Almost immediately, rumours began spreading that the Nazis themselves had set the blaze. This was not a new idea. In July AD 64, a fire swept through Rome for six days, killing hundreds and destroying two thirds of the city. The emperor Nero blamed Christians, whom he duly proceeded to persecute. But some Romans believed that Nero himself had either started the fire or let it rage, so as to cement his power and rebuild the city in his image, hence the famous story of Nero fiddling while Rome burned.

Now Hitler took on the role of Nero. Willi Münzenberg, the Communist International's master propagandist, rushed out a book, *The Brown Book of the Hitler Terror and the Burning of the Reichstag*, which claimed that Nazi stormtroopers had accessed the building through underground tunnels, lit the fire, planted van der Lubbe as a fall guy and proceeded to murder anyone who knew too much. Over the coming decades, many people would go to great lengths, including forging documents and smearing witnesses, to prove Münzenberg's theory correct.

There seemed to be some circumstantial evidence – the tunnels did exist and Göring arrived suspiciously quickly – but mostly it just felt right. The Nazis were known to be violent, deceitful and ruthless in their pursuit of power. They frequently invented fictional outrages in order to justify whatever action they wanted to take. And there was the principle of *cui bono*: whom does it benefit? The fire gave Hitler the perfect opportunity to grant himself dictatorial powers in the name of national security. As he told a British reporter on the scene:

'God grant that this be the work of the Communists. You are now witnessing the beginning of a great new epoch in German history.' So it seemed entirely plausible that he would have brought it about.

But *cui bono* is an idea, not a rule. Say you are a world-class sprinter whose most formidable rival tears her hamstring shortly before the Olympics and has to pull out of the race. You certainly benefit, but that does not necessarily mean you were personally responsible. In fact, that would be extremely unlikely. You were just very lucky. As Richard J. Evans laid out in *The Hitler Conspiracies*, Hitler was probably just very lucky.

The Führer served as a kind of conspiracy theory nexus. He was the target of one while simultaneously initiating several of his own. He claimed, for instance, that van der Lubbe was the agent of a communist plot. During the March election campaign, he insisted that a decisive Nazi victory was the only safeguard against a communist revolution. In reality, there was little prospect of such a thing, but the spectre empowered Hitler to have thousands of socialists and communists beaten, imprisoned, tortured and killed.

Evans categorised the Reichstag fire as a classic event conspiracy theory: the belief that a politically consequential event must have been planned in advance at the highest level and could not have been the work of a solitary nobody; that the subsequent death of anyone who was even remotely connected to the event must have been part of a cover-up; that the forgery of evidence is justified in pursuit of a greater truth; and that to believe otherwise is to exonerate evildoers and become complicit in the conspiracy. But van der Lubbe repeatedly confessed to starting the blaze on his own in order to incite rebellion against Nazi rule. Nine decades later, there is still no compelling evidence to suggest that he did not.

Conspiracism was the soil from which Nazism grew. Hitler owed his rise to the paranoid notion that Germany had not been militarily defeated in the First World War but betrayed by socialists, liberals and Jews back home: the stab-in-the-back myth. Two days before Germany surrendered, a newspaper claimed that 'the war of 1914 was begun by international Jewry, international freemasonry and international plutocracy, then carried through for a distinct aim: to annihilate the German empire'.

Between the wars, the *Protocols of the Elders of Zion* competed with anti-Masonic conspiracist tracts such as *World Freemasonry – World Revolution – World Republic* by Friedrich Wichtl. Proponents of the Jewish–Masonic superconspiracy could not agree on whether the Jews were manipulating the Masons or vice versa, only that the two groups were definitely in cahoots. In 1927, Erich Ludendorff, the First World War general, early Nazi ally and primary author of the stab-in-the-back myth, argued in *Annihilation of the Freemasons by Unveiling Their Secrets* that 'the "mystery" of Freemasonry is everywhere the Jew himself'. The Nazis would later ban Freemasonry and send thousands of Masons to concentration camps. There was even a special section of the Nazi elite guard, the SS, dedicated to rooting them out. SS leader Heinrich Himmler, who had read Wichtl's book as a teenager, declared that the Nazis were up against 'international Bolshevism run by the Jews and Freemasons'.

The chief co-writer of Hitler's antisemitic narrative was Alfred Rosenberg. Born in Estonia, he came to Germany in November 1918 as a White Russian exile with a copy of the *Protocols* in his suitcase. Two months later, he was one of the first people to join the German Workers' Party, which became the Nazi Party. In 1923, Hitler appointed him editor of the party newspaper, the *Völkischer Beobachter*. Rosenberg later published *The Myth of the Twentieth Century*, a work of racist pseudo-scholarship that claimed the Aryan race included Jesus and the citizens of Atlantis. Though Hitler privately considered it 'a relapse into medieval notions', his public endorsement helped it sell a million copies.

Hitler preferred his own brand of mystical nonsense: 'The trend of development which we are now experiencing would, if allowed to go on unhampered, lead to the realization of the Pan-Jewish prophecy that the Jews will one day devour the other nations and become lords of the earth.' In his frenzied mind, the Jews simultaneously controlled the machinery of international finance, the media *and* Marxism. Quoting the German philosopher Arthur Schopenhauer, Hitler called the Jew 'the Great Master of Lies'.

Conspiracy theorists are often guilty of projecting their own pernicious qualities – deceit, hatred, obsession – onto their imagined opponents. The supposed conspirator is the doppelgänger of the conspiracist, the black mirror. In this way, Hitler advanced the objectively absurd notion that the Jews planned to exterminate the Gentiles in order to justify his own genocidal impulses. Only a final victory, secured by merciless violence, could thwart the plot. The obvious vulnerability and disunity of Europe's Jews in the face of Nazi persecution could not dispel the fantasy of a formidably well-oiled conspiracy because that fantasy was the essence of Nazism. But if any single person attempted to put into practice the plan for world conquest outlined in the *Protocols*, it was Hitler himself. To all intents and purposes, he was the conspiracy.

After the war, SS major Dieter Wisliceny explained that Nazi antisemitism was fundamentally apocalyptic, based on the 'mystical-religious conception that sees the world as governed by good and evil forces'. The Aryans had been created by 'race-mystics' to combat the 'evil principle' embodied by the Jews. The Second World War was supposed to be Armageddon.

Even after his suicide in April 1945, Hitler continued to inspire conspiracy theories, from the rumour that he had faked his death and escaped to South America to the obscene industry of Holocaust denial. 'Revisionist' scholars argue that the planned extermination of six million Jews was either exaggerated or wholly fabricated, despite mountains of documentary evidence and survivor testimonies. *Cui bono*? According to the pioneering American denier Harry Elmer Barnes, it was the Allies, who wanted to deflect attention from their own war crimes, and the Israelis, 'who derive billions of [Deutschmarks] from nonexistent, mythical and imaginary cadavers'. Holocaust denial is the only conspiracy theory to have been outlawed in several countries, including Germany, Poland and Israel.

Despite his closeness to Hitler, Oswald Mosley, founder of the British Union of Fascists, later mocked the whole idea of a Jewish plot. In his 1968 autobiography *My Life*, he wrote that the notion of 'a world conspiracy run by the Jews . . . always seems to me the most complete nonsense . . . Anyone who knows how difficult it is to keep a secret among three men – particularly if they are married – knows how absurd is the idea of a world-wide secret conspiracy consciously controlling all mankind by its financial power; in real, clear analysis these deep plots are seldom anything more sinister than the usual vast muddle.'

Mosley was an antisemite but not a conspiracy theorist. William Guy Carr, the anti-communist author of 1955's *The Red Fog Over America*, was a conspiracy theorist but not an overt antisemite. In one of the worst arguments against antisemitism ever constructed, he complained that an obsession with Jews 'plays right into the hands of the Illuminati'. Hitler was both an antisemite and a conspiracy theorist, each toxic belief feeding the other, all the way to Auschwitz.

Some scholars of conspiracy theories argue that they are the fantasies of political losers: powerless to shape history, the anxious and dispossessed write their own. But Hitler was a conspiracy theorist even while he was one of the most powerful people in the world. And so was Joseph Stalin.

Karl Marx was one of the first writers to explicitly reject conspiracy theories, which he saw as a dangerous distraction from the truth about capitalism. In the second volume of *Capital*, published in 1885, he hoped to 'convince a Vulgar Marxist that Marxism does not explain depressions by the conspiracy of big business'. They were, he insisted, inherent to capitalism 'independently of good or bad intentions'. The problem with capitalism was the system, not a clique of malevolent individuals with top hats and bags full of money. (The Austrian politician Ferdinand Kronawetter made a similar point when, four years later, he called antisemitism the 'socialism of fools': blaming Jews for systemic injustices.) Unfortunately, Karl Popper wrote a century later, this had 'been forgotten by his latter-day followers, the Vulgar Marxists, who have put forward a popular conspiracy theory of society which is no better than Goebbels' myth of the Learned Elders of Zion'.

After the Russian Revolution of 1917, Lenin claimed, not

unfairly, that foreign powers were scheming to bring down the Soviet Union and also, rather less fairly, that all internal resistance to Bolshevism was due to the machinations of England and France. He had plenty of rhetorical material to use – anti-communists like Winston Churchill loudly called for Western intervention to crush the Bolsheviks – but in truth very little was done. Quite the opposite, in fact. US food aid during the famine of 1921–22 stepped in to protect Russians when the state failed, saving millions of lives. But reality had little impact on perception. The idea that the Soviet Union's problems could be pinned on the West had taken root. As is often the case, the Bolsheviks were both targets and practitioners of conspiracy theories.

Stalin, who succeeded Lenin in 1924, was a true paranoiac who saw enemies all around him. Unable to take responsibility for the human cost of his Five-Year Plan to industrialise the USSR at punishing speed, he blamed traitors and saboteurs for every disaster, from industrial accidents to famines. His arch-villain was his former rival Leon Trotsky, who had been living in exile since 1929 after denouncing Stalin as the 'gravedigger of the revolution'. In *Animal Farm* and *Nineteen Eighty-Four*, George Orwell represented the Stalinist caricature of Trotsky as a kind of evil phantom with superhuman powers, like the witches of Salem: 'some kind of invisible influence, pervading the air about them and menacing them with all kinds of dangers'.

Stalin's paranoia – partly genuine, partly a political strategy – culminated in the Great Terror. The assassination of the Soviet official Sergei Kirov in Leningrad in 1934 gave him the excuse to purge the Communist Party of every foe, real or imagined, starting with the leading Bolsheviks favoured by Lenin. Grigory Zinoviev and Lev Kamenev were immediately accused of directing Kirov's assassin, although there is no evidence that he was ever more than a lone gunman.

In a series of show trials between 1936 and 1938, these men and more were accused of plotting with Trotsky to commit terrorism, conduct sabotage, wreck the economy, forge alliances with Nazi Germany and Japan and assassinate Soviet leaders, including Stalin himself. 'Experience teaches that the masses must be given for all difficult and complicated processes a simple, easily grasped explanation,' says the Soviet interrogator in *Darkness at Noon*, Arthur Koestler's 1940 novel about the trials. 'According to what I know of history, I see that mankind could never do without scapegoats.' Stalin had the rare power to make reality appear to conform to his conspiracy theories. The accused were tortured into confessing to these imaginary crimes, again like the Salem 'witches'. Georgy Pyatakov, for example, confessed to complicity in 'counter-revolution of the most vile, loathsome, fascist type, Trotskyite counter-revolution' before he was found guilty and shot in the back of the head. Trotsky himself quipped that these alleged plots 'all took place in the fourth dimension'.

Why did innocent people co-sign their own death sentences? Some defendants confessed to save their families, who were then persecuted anyway. Others, conditioned by years of loyalty to Stalin, seem to have convinced themselves that they were indeed guilty in some way. In the West, most communists had invested too much in the USSR's success to allow themselves to doubt the legitimacy of the show trials, and would rather become conspiracy theorists themselves than believe that Stalin was a deceitful murderer.

Stalin did not just pursue prominent Bolsheviks. During the late 1920s and early 1930s, he targeted the kulaks. This term had originally indicated a wealthier peasant, but as the

Soviet regime failed its people in ever more heinous ways, it could be applied to anyone the authorities wanted to blame for their own negligence. 'The kulaks stood between us and the good life,' party loyalist Pasha Angelina wrote. Stalin eventually ordered their liquidation as a class, resulting in the deaths of millions.

Workers who had been in the vicinity of industrial accidents were arrested on charges of sabotage. Under Stalin, there was no such thing as accident or incompetence, and certainly not error on his part. Stalin also targeted ethnic minorities, particularly Poles, executing some 250,000 people for alleged espionage. His paranoia filled mass graves.

Bizarrely, the one person he did not suspect of plotting against him was Hitler. Hidden away, surrounded by sycophants, he cut himself off from other sources of information. Right up until the very moment that Hitler broke the Nazi–Soviet pact and invaded the Soviet Union, on 22 June 1941, Stalin dismissed reports of an imminent attack as 'clumsy fabrications' by British intelligence. Indeed, when an ex-communist soldier deserted German forces the day before and swam across a river to inform the Russians of an impending Nazi invasion, Stalin had him shot for spreading 'disinformation'. His error demonstrates that paranoia is not omnidirectional; it runs along certain narrative grooves that have been carved by the conspiracy theorist's biases.

Stalin included Jews in his nationalist purges. After briefly supporting the establishment of Israel on the faulty assumption that it would be a Soviet ally in the Middle East, he became explicitly anti-Zionist and increasingly paranoid about Jewish influence. In 1951, he personally scripted the show trial of 11 Jewish communists accused of espionage and sabotage in Czechoslovakia. In January 1953, two months before his death, he came up with the conspiracy theory known as the 'Doctors' Plot', in which Jewish doctors were allegedly murdering Soviet leaders on behalf of Israel and the US. Had he lived, it is very likely that Stalin would have launched a massive campaign against Russian Jews, based on imaginary crimes.

Hannah Arendt, a scholar of totalitarianism, observed that both Stalin and Hitler had been trained in covert action: Hitler as an undercover agent for the German army and Stalin in the conspiratorial wing of the Bolsheviks. She characterised each regime as 'a secret society in broad daylight', with an 'unsurpassed capacity to establish and safeguard the fictitious world through consistent lying'. The object of conspiracy theories, she wrote, 'was always to reveal official history as a joke, to demonstrate a sphere of secret influences in which the visible, traceable and known historical reality was only the outward façade erected explicitly to fool the people'. If history is a forgery anyway, they implied, it 'might as well be the playground of crackpots'.

The manufacture and dissemination of conspiracy theories remained part of Soviet foreign policy throughout the Cold War. After Israel defeated Soviet-backed Arab nations in the Six-Day War of 1967, the Soviets revived old antisemitic conspiracy theories with a focus on Zionism, rather than Jews per se – a euphemistic bait-and-switch that has been used by some on the left ever since. Until this point, Israel had been regarded as a tool of US imperialism. Now it was reimagined as the secret power behind it – America's puppets were now its puppet-masters. According to one document: 'An extensive network of Zionist organisations with a common center, a common program, and funds much greater than those of the Mafia "Cosa Nostra" is active behind the scenes of the international theater.' It was the *Protocols* with a newfangled Cold War makeover.

One Soviet conspiracy theory proved fatal. In the early 1980s, when the US government was cruelly slow to address the AIDS crisis, rumours spread in the Black and gay communities that the virus was a military bioweapon that had been developed with genocidal intent. Agents of the KGB and the East German Stasi propagated the conspiracy theory 'in order to strengthen anti-American sentiments in the world and to spark domestic political controversies in the USA', according to a 1986 East German memo. The consequences were appalling. Those who disbelieved the scientific explanation for the origins of AIDS were far less likely to take medication or precautions. South African president Thabo Mbeki's belief in AIDS conspiracy theories led him to delay the rollout of antiretroviral therapies, at an estimated cost of 330,000 lives. Few lies in history have been so unintentionally devastating.

Stalin's paranoia, though not his murderous violence, was mirrored by anti-communists in the US during the early years of the Cold War. Opponents of President Roosevelt's New Deal had already accused him of communism and even secret Jewishness: some referred to 'Rosenfelt' and the 'Jew Deal'. The breakdown of the wartime alliance with Stalin – and the discovery that the Soviets had used that alliance to plant spies in the heart of US institutions – injected rocket fuel into the belief that America was riddled with communists.

This Red Scare began in 1947, driven by the House Un-American Activities Committee, but took on the name of its most energetic self-promoter: McCarthyism. Senator Joseph McCarthy of Wisconsin had been casting around for a career-boosting gimmick for a few years before he alighted on anti-communism. On 9 February 1950, in a speech to the Republican Women's Club of Wheeling, West Virginia, he waved a piece of paper and claimed to 'have here in my hand' a list of 205 Communist Party members working in the State Department. Without realising it, McCarthy was echoing Jedediah Morse, who boasted in 1799 that 'I have now in my possession' a list of names of powerful members of the Illuminati. In fact, McCarthy had no such list – not one single name – and quickly downgraded his claim to 57 people. But that did not matter. He had launched himself onto the public stage as a fearless crusader against communism.

McCarthyism is an example of moulding a conspiracy theory around the bones of a real conspiracy. There had certainly been genuine plots by communist spies, whose achievements included stealing the secrets of the atomic bomb. But by the time McCarthy arrived on the scene, the spies had all either returned home or been caught, so he was left with an army of phantoms. It is no coincidence that the 1950s saw the first wave of hysteria about UFOs and literal aliens living among us. Paranoia was rampant, but it lacked a legitimate target.

Rather than pursuing minor civil servants, McCarthy went straight to the top. In 1949, China had fallen to Mao Zedong's communists and the Soviets had tested their first atomic bomb. In 1950, the Korean War had begun and former State Department official Alger Hiss had been convicted of perjury during an earlier trial for espionage. For McCarthy, these blows to national security demanded a scapegoat at the highest level – something commensurate with their gravity. So he accused President Truman's Secretary of Defense, the war hero George Marshall, of sabotaging US foreign policy for the benefit of communists in Russia and China. 'How can we account for our present situation unless we believe that men high in this government are concerting to deliver us to disaster?' he asked Congress in 1951. 'This must be the product of a great conspiracy, a conspiracy so immense as to dwarf any previous such venture in the history of man.' Like Stalin, he could not attribute political setbacks to incompetence, bad luck or external factors. They could only be evidence of a wicked and treasonous plot. And the greater the scale of the setback, the greater the scale of the plot.

Ordinary red-baiting politicians like Richard Nixon denounced all progressive policies as socialistic – a crude tactic that is still used today by the American right. But McCarthy went a step further. He accused politicians and officials, Democrat and Republican alike, of being actual communists. The more outrageous his claims were, the more attention he got. McCarthy whipped up a storm of smears, allegations and fabricated 'facts', which the press dutifully reported because it was considered bad form to fact-check a senator's words. Whenever a newspaper did criticise him, McCarthy accused it of being part of the communist conspiracy and carried on as before. As ever, the rebuttal of a conspiracy theory served only to prove to its adherents how widespread and powerful the conspiracy had become. According to McCarthy's biographer, David M. Oshinsky: 'The senator provided a simple explanation for America's decline in the world. He spoke of a massive internal conspiracy, directed by Communists and abetted by government officials . . . He provided names, documents and statistics – in short, the *appearance* of diligent research.' McCarthy was an adept pseudo-scholar.

For Richard Hofstadter, McCarthy was the classic postwar example of the paranoid style. 'At times politics becomes an arena into which the wildest fancies are projected, the most paranoid suspicions, the most absurd superstitions, the most bizarre apocalyptic fantasies,' he wrote in 1955. He was horrified that the press and public had been forced to take seriously characters like McCarthy, who 'project into the arena of politics utterly irrelevant fantasies and disorders of a purely personal kind'.

Arthur Miller cleverly used the Salem witch trials as an allegory for McCarthyism in his 1953 play *The Crucible*. Communists, unlike witches, did exist but not in the manner that McCarthy claimed they did. During his three and a half years on the national stage, he did not expose a single Soviet spy or informant.

After McCarthy's career ended in disgrace in 1954, the Red Scare baton passed to Robert Welch, a retired candy manufacturer who founded the right-wing John Birch Society and considered communism 'a gigantic conspiracy to enslave mankind'. He named the group after a US military intelligence officer whose murder by Chinese communists in 1945 had kicked off 'a struggle from which either Communism or Christian-style civilization must emerge with one completely triumphant and the other completely destroyed'. It was Armageddon all over again.

Like McCarthy, Welch was not a man to hold back. This is the most generous possible formulation for a man who was completely untroubled by logic, evidence or moral restraint. In his view, communists had been controlling US policy and capturing its institutions since 1933. He claimed that President Dwight Eisenhower, a Republican and a war hero, was without doubt 'a dedicated, conscious agent of the Communist conspiracy', as was his Secretary of State, John Foster Dulles. In 1962, Welch predicted that within a decade Chinese communists would have occupied the United

States and herded Americans into concentration camps. To give their ravings the appearance of historical legitimacy, the Birchers revived the work of earlier conspiracy theorists, from John Robison and Augustin Barruel to Nesta Webster. Needless to say, Welch was a great believer in the Illuminati.

Who knew how far the conspiracy extended? An evangelical leader, David A. Noebel, maintained that 'four mop-headed anti-Christ beatniks' were destroying the minds of American teenagers on behalf of communism. These were the Beatles. The Bircher Dr Joseph Crow theorised that the technical sophistication of the band's post-1966 material could only be explained by the fact that it had been 'put together by behavioral scientists in some "think tank" in order to promote promiscuity, drug addiction and revolution'. The possibility that they were growing in creative confidence or had more time to experiment in the studio once they stopped touring did not seem to have occurred to him. The Bircher belief that water fluoridation was part of the communist plot was memorably parodied in Stanley Kubrick's *Dr Strangelove* by the deranged general raving about 'precious bodily fluids'. Even the libertarian writer Ayn Rand, though a fanatical anti-communist herself, found the John Birch Society's worldview 'childishly naïve and superficial'.

The 1964 presidential campaign of the ultra-conservative senator Barry Goldwater brought the Bircher worldview into the Republican Party. In her book *A Choice Not an Echo*, Goldwater supporter Phyllis Schlafly claimed that every Republican nominee for the last 30 years had been chosen by a conspiracy of bankers, journalists, intellectuals and fake conservatives in order to lose to the Democrats. 'Most of what is ascribed to "accident" or "coincidence" is really the result of human plans,' she claimed, in a pithy summary of the conspiracy theorist worldview.

The Bircher Gary Allen also derided the idea of unplanned events in *None Dare Call It Conspiracy*, his influential 1971 bestseller, which attacked bankers, communists and the descendants of the Illuminati. 'Politicians and "intellectuals" are attracted to the concept that events are propelled by some mysterious tide of history or happen by accident,' he wrote. 'In our opinion, nothing is more simplistic than doggedly holding onto the accidental view of major world events.' As David Icke later said: 'I'll call myself a conspiracy theorist if you call yourself a coincidence theorist.'

This kind of thinking would take decades to consume the Republican Party entirely, but it began with McCarthy and never went away. In a November 1961 speech, President Kennedy poked fun at the paranoid right: 'There have always been those on the fringes of our society who have sought to escape their own responsibility by finding a simple solution, an appealing slogan or a convenient scapegoat. Financial crises could be explained by the presence of too many immigrants or too few greenbacks. War could be attributed to munitions makers or international bankers. Peace conferences failed because we were duped by the British, or tricked by the French, or deceived by the Russians . . . At times these fanatics have achieved a temporary success among those who lack the will or the wisdom to face unpleasant facts or unsolved problems. But in time the basic good sense and stability of the great American consensus has always prevailed.'

Two years later, Kennedy would be dead, and his murder would inspire the most famous event conspiracy theory of all time.

CHAPTER THREE
JFK and the Event Conspiracy Theory

Richard Hofstadter first delivered 'The Paranoid Style in American Politics' as a lecture on 21 November 1963, the day before the assassination of President Kennedy in Dallas, Texas. But even when he published a revised version in *Harper's* in November 1964, after the Warren Commission had presented its final report into the murder, he barely mentioned Kennedy. Hofstadter's argument was that the paranoid style was overwhelmingly a phenomenon of the American right, and the right did not like Kennedy very much. The JFK assassination revealed something disturbing that contradicted his theory. The left was also susceptible to the paranoid style. And they were getting into it in a big way.

As Oliver Stone, the director of 1991's conspiracist blockbuster *JFK*, said, this was 'the most thoroughly documented crime in American history'. It is the conspiracy theory that you, the reader, are statistically most likely to believe. On the sixtieth anniversary, 65 per cent of US adults told Gallup that they thought Lee Harvey Oswald did not work alone. Yet it is not in fact one single theory but a tangle of often mutually contradictory ones, like paranoid spaghetti. While most people are sceptical of the official narrative, they cannot agree on what they think *did* happen.

To put it as objectively as possible: at 12.30 p.m. on 22 November 1963, President Kennedy was struck by at least two bullets while travelling in a motorcade through Dealey Plaza in Dallas. Texas governor John Connally, who was riding in the same limousine, was also hit. The final bullet ripped off the top of Kennedy's head. The president was pronounced dead at Parkland Memorial Hospital at 1.00 p.m.

The immediate assumption was that the killer was a right-wing extremist radicalised by the John Birch Society. Texas was a conservative state, and concerns about the radical right had been mounting. 'What happened?' former vice-president Richard Nixon asked FBI director J. Edgar Hoover. 'Was it one of those right-wing nuts?' But less than an hour later, Dallas police arrested 24-year-old former Marine Lee Harvey Oswald in a movie theatre. Initially, this was for shooting a police officer, but he was quickly tied to the assassination.

On the face of it, Oswald looked as guilty as the Reichstag arsonist Marinus van der Lubbe. He worked at the Dallas Book Depository, which was the source of the shots. Investigators found a 6.5 mm Mannlicher–Carcano bolt-action rifle on the sixth floor of the depository that bore Oswald's palm print and fibres from his shirt. Bullet fragments in Kennedy's limousine were matched to the Carcano. A construction worker, Howard Brennan, had a clear view of the sixth floor and saw a man matching Oswald's description take the final shot.

But unlike van der Lubbe, Oswald denied the crime. He insisted that he was being made a 'patsy' due to his being a pro-Cuba Marxist who had lived in the Soviet Union between 1959 and 1962. Two days later, he was shot dead at a Dallas police station by nightclub owner Jack Ruby, live on national television. There would be no trial, no confession, no clear motive.

A week after the assassination of Kennedy, Gallup found that fewer than one in three Americans believed that Oswald had acted alone and more than half believed in some kind of plot. But perhaps this could be attributed to sheer disbelief that a disturbed nobody with a mail-order rifle could take down the most powerful man in the world, rather than a widespread conspiracy theory.

In December, a young left-wing lawyer, Mark Lane, really set the conspiracist ball rolling with an article in the *National Guardian* that criticised the assumption of Oswald's guilt. Lane established the Citizens' Committee of Inquiry to interview witnesses and collect evidence. In the UK, the philosopher and peer Bertrand Russell set up the Who Killed Kennedy Committee, which included such luminaries as the future Labour Party leader Michael Foot, the theatre critic Kenneth Tynan and the historian Hugh Trevor-Roper. This was a serious business, operating at the highest level of cultural and intellectual life.

Meanwhile, an official commission headed by Chief Justice Earl Warren was frantically assembling evidence for what would become an 888-page report. Some members worried that whatever conclusions they came to, the report would only create more controversy. They were to be proved entirely right. When the report was released to the public on 27 September 1964, finding that both Oswald and Ruby had acted alone, conspiracy theorists immediately perceived it as the cover-up that proved the crime. Under pressure to reach a unanimous conclusion before the November election, and hampered by the CIA's reluctance to cooperate, the commission had left many inconsistencies unaddressed and alternative perpetrators unexplored. Ironically, though, its critics largely relied on the commission's own published evidence, which ran to 27 volumes and 10.4 million words, to discredit it. You might imagine that a proper cover-up would have suppressed any inconvenient evidence and that the holes in the report made it less, not more, likely to be a whitewash. But according to the conspiracy theorists, you would be wrong.

Unlike the Warren Commission's interviewees, the doubters were not experts in ballistics or autopsies, but enthusiastic amateurs on a crusade to save America. 'Can we continue to live a lie about what happened in Dallas on November 22, 1963,' asked Richard H. Popkin, a historian of religion, 'or has the time come to face what it means and what it involves for all of us?'

In 1966, when 50 per cent of Americans said that they disbelieved the commission's conclusions, Popkin's *The Second Oswald* and Lane's *Rush to Judgment* were in the vanguard of a whole new industry of JFK scholarship, which sucked in mainstream titles like the *New York Review of Books* and the *New Republic*. The avalanche of theories injected new phrases into the national vocabulary: magic bullet, lone gunman, grassy knoll. The alleged plotters included the CIA, the FBI, the KGB, the Mafia, Cuba's Fidel Castro, Cuban exiles who hated Castro, Texan oil moguls, the military-industrial complex, the Ku Klux Klan and President Lyndon B. Johnson. The great debunker Vincent Bugliosi once calculated that the cast of suspects included 42 groups, 82 assassins and 214 co-conspirators. As the historian Stephen E. Ambrose quipped about the JFK industry: 'They posit conspiracies involving so many men that their meetings would have had to be held in Madison Square Garden.'

One technique of conspiracy theorists is to smother the reader in data so that it becomes very hard for a non-expert to separate facts from speculation. Another tactic is to present the most esoteric theories as plausible and the most likely explanations as not just improbable but impossible. Any flaw in the Warren Report was damning while any inconsistency in an alternative thesis was brushed over. In the language of conspiracy theories, to say that a detail is 'odd' or 'curious' or 'surprising' is to imply that it must be suspicious. But life itself is frequently odd, curious and surprising.

Several elements of the case that once seemed like damning evidence turned out not to be. They help illuminate the conspiracist state of mind.

The lone gunman. JFK conspiracy theorists contend that it is absurdly unlikely that someone as powerless and unknown as Oswald could have killed someone as powerful and famous as the president. The dissonance is unbearable. But solitary assassins with grudges and/or mental health problems have killed Presidents Abraham Lincoln (1865), James A. Garfield (1881) and William McKinley (1901), and wounded Presidents Theodore Roosevelt (1912) and Ronald Reagan (1981). Seven months before Dealey Plaza, Oswald himself attempted to assassinate Edwin Walker, a prominent member of the John Birch Society, with the same Carcano rifle.

The three bullets. The bedrock of any JFK conspiracy theory is the alleged impossibility of Oswald firing off three shots (the first missed) in the space of a few seconds, and the further impossibility of one of those bullets passing through Kennedy's body into Governor Connally. It therefore follows that the kill shot came from somewhere else, probably the infamous grassy knoll, a small hill overlooking Dealey Plaza. Even President Johnson expressed disbelief about the so-called 'magic bullet'. But Oswald was a decent marksman, and numerous reconstructions and computer models have since demonstrated that he could indeed have fired three shots within 7.1 seconds. Because the limousine's seats were not level, the 'magic bullet' could easily have penetrated both men.

Back and to the left. Fans of Oliver Stone's *JFK* will recall the famous courtroom scene where New Orleans District Attorney Jim Garrison (played by Kevin Costner) rewinds Abraham Zapruder's amateur footage of the assassination to show that although Kennedy was allegedly shot in the back of the head, the top of his head was blown backwards, so there must have been a second gunman in front of him. But later analysis of the footage with new technology showed that Kennedy's head did in fact pitch forward momentarily before an exploding nerve ending rocked it back.

Mysterious bystanders. Certain suspicious figures captured in photographs or the Zapruder film became key characters in conspiracist lore. One was the man seen opening an umbrella, despite the sunny weather, as Kennedy's limousine approached. He was never identified or interviewed by the Warren Commission. Perhaps he was signalling to the assassin(s)? Then there were the 'three tramps' photographed under police escort near the book depository after the shooting. Various theorists have claimed they were contract killers or CIA agents. But there are answers to both these mysteries. In 1978, a man called Louie Steven Witt came forward and explained that he had waved the umbrella as a protest. Because Kennedy's father Joe had endorsed appeasing Hitler in the 1930s, Witt was referencing the umbrella-bearing, pro-appeasement British prime minister Neville Chamberlain. And the three suspicious tramps have been identified as, well, three homeless men.

The badge man. In 1983, the curator of the museum at the Texas School Book Depository studied a Polaroid of the assassination by spectator Mary Moorman and detected the figure of a man in a police uniform with a glinting badge, his face obscured by a muzzle flash. Could this be another assassin? No, because he never existed. David Lifton, a leading JFK researcher, eventually admitted that he had perceived a figure where there was really only a blur – most likely sunlight reflecting off a Coke bottle. He wondered, with commendable self-awareness, 'How certain could I be that my basic processes of perception were not hopelessly biased?'

Dead witnesses. In 1967, the *Sunday Times* claimed that the odds of 18 people connected to the assassination – including reporters, CIA agents and friends of the president – dying in the space of three years without foul play were 100,000 trillion to one. That extraordinary figure was widely quoted and made for a chilling conclusion to the 1973 docudrama *Executive Action*, based on a book by Mark Lane. But the paper had made an elementary mathematical error, which it immediately corrected. The journalist had asked an actuary to give the odds for 18 specific people dying, which were obviously extremely low. But the likelihood of *any* 18 people out of the 2,479 names in the Warren Commission index dying was as high as 83 per cent. By 1976, as many as 101 people with some connection to the murder had died, but most died of natural causes, years after the event, and were only tangentially linked. There was nothing statistically abnormal in the pattern of deaths. If you look instead at the much larger number of survivors whose testimonies were far more important, the logic of the cover-up becomes unfathomable.

In each case, JFK researchers either disbelieved the explanations or moved on to the next piece of suspicious evidence, never losing faith in the essential truth of their theories. As the belief in a conspiracy became an article of faith on the left, some progressives warned that it could lead to dark places. The veteran journalist I. F. Stone complained that he had dedicated himself to combating 'conspiracy theories of history, character assassination, guilt by association and demonology' on the anti-communist right, only to see the left 'using these same tactics'. The historian Henry Steele Commager warned of a new 'conspiracy psychology': 'a feeling that great events can't be explained by ordinary processes . . . We are on the road to a paranoid explanation of things . . . There's some psychological requirement that forces [people] to reject the ordinary, and find refuge in the extraordinary.'

Dealey Plaza was the watershed for American conspiracy theories.

After Dallas came the assassinations of Malcolm X in 1965 and Martin Luther King and Robert F. Kennedy in 1968, all against the backcloth of the disastrous war in Vietnam. Inevitably, people looked for connections. Some conspiracy theories were harmlessly bizarre. One posited that Paul McCartney had died in 1966 and been replaced by a lookalike, but that the other Beatles, for some inexplicable reason, insisted on hiding clues to the death in their songs and artwork. But whether they were grave or frivolous, all these theories were a post-JFK phenomenon. Suddenly everything was suspect.

While *Executive Action* was a dud, a more generalised anxiety about state-sponsored assassinations, secret meetings, murdered witnesses and epic cover-ups produced a golden age of paranoid art in America. In hauntingly pessimistic thrillers like *The Parallax View* and *Three Days of the Condor*, the heroic investigators wound up either dead or despairing of ever exposing the conspiracy. 'If the picture works,' *The Parallax View* director Alan J. Pakula told his star Warren Beatty, 'the audience will trust the person next to them a little less.'

The line between fact and fiction became blurred. Even those who tried to mock conspiracy theories found themselves incorporated into them. In 1975, Robert Shea and Robert Anton Wilson began publishing the *Illuminatus!* trilogy, a mischievous parody of conspiracy theories that involved Nazis, Atlantis and multiple assassins simultaneously vying to kill JFK, based on some of the weirder letters they had received while working at *Playboy* magazine. They ended up inadvertently helping to revive the Illuminati mythology that they were spoofing. In 1977, a clever British mock-documentary, *Alternative 3*, purported to reveal a secret plan to build an off-world colony to escape the earth's imminent environmental collapse. The credits revealed that it wasn't real, but a tie-in book was seriously taken up by conspiracy theorists in the US.

Pakula's follow-up to *The Parallax View* was *All the President's Men*, an Oscar-nominated hit about the Watergate investigation. The scandal seemed to confirm the era's ambient paranoia, but it was also a reminder of the messiness of real conspiracies. Although it took more than two years for the scandal to force the resignation of President Nixon, the facts of the case were ultimately quite simple. Five men connected to the Committee for the Re-Election of the President definitely broke into the Democratic National Convention's offices in Washington DC's Watergate building on the night of 17 June 1972 to repair a wiretap planted in an earlier burglary. Nixon definitely approved plans to cover up his administration's involvement in the break-in. The administration definitely weaponised the FBI, CIA and Internal Revenue Service against its political opponents. Watergate was not a conspiracy theory. It was, undeniably, a conspiracy.

Ironically, Nixon was doomed by his own conspiracist paranoia. In 1971, he had put together a covert team of 'Plumbers' to collect and leak information about people he believed were conspiring against him, especially Jews and Ivy League intellectuals. This was the squad that later broke into the Watergate building. 'We're up against an enemy,' Nixon told his chief of staff. 'A conspiracy. They're using any means. We are going to use any means. Is that clear?' He maintained an ever-growing list of enemies. Every opponent was in on the conspiracy, from student protesters ('We have to find out who controls them') to environmentalists ('What they're interested in is destroying the system'). This was the paranoia loop that led to Watergate. As Nixon later admitted: 'I was paranoiac, or almost a basket case, with regard to secrecy.'

Watergate proved that cover-ups are actually very difficult to pull off: people talk, evidence emerges, plotters fall out. But the US public's faith in politicians never recovered. In 1964, 77 per cent of Americans told Pew Research Center that they trusted their government to do the right thing most or all of the time. By 1974, the number had plunged to just 36 per cent. Many conservatives convinced themselves that Nixon himself had been a victim of a left-wing *coup d'état*.

Meanwhile, in London, another vicious circle of paranoia was playing out. Opponents of Labour prime minister Harold Wilson were gossiping that he was a Soviet agent whose predecessor as party leader, Hugh Gaitskell, had been murdered. This fiction inspired loose talk of a military coup to save the UK from communism. In response, Wilson cooked up his own conspiracy theory involving intelligence agencies from three countries. This doubling of paranoia was a Cold War ailment. James Jesus Angleton, the CIA's chief of counterintelligence between 1954 and 1975, took a phrase from T. S. Eliot's poem

'Gerontion' to characterise the looking-glass world he inhabited: a 'wilderness of mirrors'.

In their ceaseless hunt for communist conspiracies, Western intelligence agencies conspired against their own citizens. In December 1974, the investigative reporter Seymour Hersh exposed an illegal CIA operation to spy on the anti-war movement. 'Overnight, CIA became a sinister shadow organisation in the minds of the American people,' complained one high-ranking agent. 'Visions of a CIA payroll swollen with zealous and ubiquitous cloak-and-dagger villains impervious to good judgment and outside control arose throughout the country.'

Then, in 1975, the Senate's Church Committee revealed several more covert government programmes: COINTEL-PRO, which infiltrated civil rights organisations such as the Black Panthers and the American Indian Movement; MKUltra, which drugged US citizens in mind-control experiments; and Family Jewels, a CIA project to assassinate foreign leaders such as the Republic of Congo's Patrice Lumumba and Cuba's Fidel Castro. Now it was clear why the CIA had refused to cooperate fully with the Warren Commission. The findings retrospectively confirmed suspicions that might once have been dismissed as paranoid fantasies. Earlier conspiracy theories had focused on global networks of alien infiltrators but now many people felt that America itself was a plot. The historian Christopher Lasch observed a new way of thinking 'that sees government as a conspiracy against the people themselves'.

This avalanche of revelations helped to explain a new wave of interest in what the government knew about UFOs. In 1973, the Center for UFO Studies opened in Chicago. Five years later, the long-forgotten crash of an unidentified flying object in Roswell, New Mexico, in 1947 was picked up and turned into a plot to cover up an extraterrestrial landing. (The US Air Force later admitted that the object had been a military surveillance balloon.) Thanks to Watergate and the Church Committee, the ufologists found a more sympathetic audience than ever.

In 1979, the JFK researchers finally scored a win. The House Select Committee on Assassinations concluded that President Kennedy was 'probably assassinated as the result of a conspiracy' and, based on later discredited acoustical evidence, that there was probably a fourth shot from the grassy knoll. This confirmed what most people already thought. 'Next thing you know they'll be blaming World War II on Hitler,' joked talk-show host Johnny Carson. After so many real conspiracies had been exposed, it seemed naïve to believe that Kennedy's assassination wasn't another one. In 1976, the proportion of Americans who believed in a plot peaked at a staggering 81 per cent. It did not drop significantly until 2003.

In 1986, America was hit by a scandal that was arguably even more pernicious than Watergate. An Iranian official exposed a covert project by the Reagan administration to sell illegal arms to Iran and channel the revenue to right-wing Contra rebels in Nicaragua – a five-year conspiracy that flew in the face of official US policy. Iran–Contra blossomed into a huge, months-long scandal that forced Reagan to make a bizarrely phrased apology. 'A few months ago I told the American people I did not trade arms for hostages,' he said. 'My heart and my best intentions still tell me that's true, but the facts and the evidence tell me it is not.' It is always annoying when the facts contradict your heart.

The unveiling of real conspiracies shows how limited, discoverable and often incompetent they are compared to the giant plots outlined in conspiracy theories. Nonetheless, nothing feeds false conspiracy theories like proof of real conspiracies. According to the journalist Michael Kelly: 'The unfolding revelations of Iran–Contra gave a great and lasting boost to conspiratorial thinking everywhere in America: if this impossible scenario was true, then nothing was beyond credibility.'

The experience of proven skulduggery helps explain why America's largest incubator of conspiracy theories, outside of the extremes of right and left, was the Black community. The government had admitted that civil rights activists had been infiltrated, undermined, set up and murdered. In 1972, it emerged that for the last 40 years doctors at Alabama's Tuskegee Institute had deliberately withheld treatment from hundreds of Black men with syphilis, allowing many of them to die in the name of scientific inquiry.

It therefore seemed plausible that the CIA had deliberately flooded Black inner-city communities with crack cocaine, or had a 'King Alfred Plan' to put Black people into concentration camps, or had developed the AIDS virus in a military laboratory as a tool of genocide. According to one 1990 poll, one in three Black Americans believed the AIDS theory, and twice as many thought the crack theory held up. AIDS treatment and prevention, too, were suspect: the drug AZT was poison; condoms were designed to reduce the population; clean needles distributed to heroin users were a ploy to foster addiction. Advances in the diagnosis and treatment of AIDS could not dispel the myth. Among the conspiracy theorists was Barack Obama's pastor, Jeremiah Wright. 'Based on this Tuskegee experiment and based on what has happened to Africans in this country,' Wright said in 2008, 'I believe our government is capable of doing anything.'

The same logic played out after Hurricane Katrina devastated New Orleans in August 2005 and the incompetence of the Federal Emergency Management Agency (FEMA) unnecessarily prolonged the suffering of its mostly Black victims. Louis Farrakhan, leader of the fantastically paranoid Nation of Islam, claimed that the government had deliberately blown the levee to inundate poorer majority Black districts. Two months later, film director Spike Lee said on TV show *Real Time with Bill Maher* that Farrakhan's theory was 'not far-fetched'. ABC News reporter Michel Martin replied that 'anybody with any knowledge of history can understand why a lot of people can feel this way' but dismissed the theory. Lee was undeterred: 'Presidents have been assassinated. So why is that so far-fetched?'

Of course, to go from assassinations to a deliberate plan to murder hundreds of Black Americans and wreck a city was quite a cognitive leap. But the government's objective failure over Katrina, as with the AIDS crisis, destroyed trust and made anything feel possible. Through the same process, revered investigative journalists like John Pilger and Robert Fisk, who made their names during that period, eventually became conspiracy theorists who endorsed the phoney self-justifications of Vladimir Putin and Bashar al-Assad. After so many years of exposing Western hypocrisy and deceit, these proud sceptics grew credulous about any claim, however outlandish, about Western hypocrisy and deceit, because every allegation confirmed what they already believed. Their reporting decayed into insinuations, dubiously sourced claims and unproven connections.

None of these people started out as fantasists. Living through the monstrous consequences of real conspiracies made them incapable of *not* seeing a conspiracy. In 1991, the journalist Christopher Hitchens listed more than a dozen confirmed instances of scheming and deception by the US government and argued that conspiracy theories were a psychologically valid response. 'Conspiracy theory thus becomes an ailment of democracy,' he said. 'It is the white noise which moves in to fill the vacuity of the official version.'

That same year, Oliver Stone gave JFK conspiracy theories a whole new lease of life with a masterpiece of white noise.

Stone's movie *JFK* is tremendous entertainment. It is a technical masterpiece that won well-deserved Academy Awards for its cinematography and editing as well as six other nominations. And it is by far the most popular account of the Kennedy assassination, taking a quarter of a billion dollars at the box office. It is also total and unmitigated nonsense – an orgy of innuendo, supposition and deceit that too many viewers perceived as historical fact. 'The only thing [Stone] gets right in *JFK*,' scoffed Gerald Posner, the author of the anti-conspiracist book *Case Closed*, 'is the date on which Kennedy is killed.'

JFK did not create a nation of conspiracy theorists. As Kevin Costner, who played District Attorney Jim Garrison, reportedly said: 'Nobody in America believes Oswald did it.' But it is a peerless demonstration of how it *feels* to be a conspiracy theorist: the obsessive accumulation of data, the wild deductive leaps, the disbelief in coincidence and the spinning of hair-raising yarns. '*JFK* is a brilliant reflection of our unease and paranoia, our restless dissatisfaction,' wrote the film critic Roger Ebert. 'On that level, it is completely factual.'

JFK is a movie made by a conspiracy theorist, based on books by two conspiracy theorists, in consultation with other conspiracy theorists. Stone's gateway into the story was *On the Trail of the Assassins*, one of Garrison's three books about the assassination. Until he read it, Stone said, 'I thought that people like Mark Lane were crazy. I thought Lee Oswald had shot the president.' Not any more. He asked the book's editor, Zachary Sklar, to co-write the screenplay for *JFK*.

In 1969, Garrison had prosecuted New Orleans business-man Clay Shaw, played by Tommy Lee Jones in the movie, for allegedly conspiring to assassinate Kennedy as part of a CIA *coup d'état*. To this day it is the only criminal prosecution brought in connection with the assassination. During the trial, Garrison became the first person to screen the Zapruder film to members of the public. (It wasn't shown on TV until 1975.) He said exciting things like: 'The key to the whole case is through the looking glass. Black is white; white is black.'

In real life, rather than *JFK*, Garrison's case was so weak that the jury deliberated for less than an hour before unani-mously acquitting Shaw. One juror said it would have taken less time but they had to incorporate toilet breaks. Harry Connick Sr, who replaced Garrison as district attorney in 1973, said that the prosecution was 'one of the grossest, most extreme miscarriages of justice in the annals of American judicial history'. *Newsweek* called the trial 'a merry kind of parody of conspiracy theories, a can-you-top-this of arbitrarily conjoined improbabilities'. Garrison was found to have bribed and drugged witnesses and concealed evidence.

Whenever Garrison's credibility was challenged, though, Stone would retort that the case against Clay Shaw was just one strand of his movie. This was true. JFK researchers are notoriously disunited. They all have their own theories and they cannot agree on anything except their contempt for the Warren Commission. Rather than pick one theory, Stone combined as many as possible into a hectic megamix in which nothing was discounted. His film is a kind of JFK bingo, ticking off all the key ingredients from the Mafia and the CIA to the grassy knoll and the umbrella man, with overwhelming velocity and cinematic skill.

Stone's other main source was *Crossfire: The Plot That Killed Kennedy*, by the journalist Jim Marrs. According to Marrs, a conspiracy of 'powerful men in the leadership of US military, banking, Government, intelligence and organized-crime circles ordered their faithful agents to manipulate Mafia-Cuban-[CIA] Agency pawns to kill the chief'. It might have been quicker to say who *wasn't* in on it. Marrs's subsequent work included *Rule by Secrecy: The Hidden History That Connects the Trilateral Commission, the Freemasons, and the Great Pyramids* and *The Rise of the Fourth Reich: The Secret Societies That Threaten to Take Over America*. He also wrote books about the Illuminati, the New World Order, 9/11 and UFOs. In short, he was not just somebody with valid concerns about the Warren Report. He was a grade-A crank.

As for Mark Lane, the original JFK truther, he led what we might generously call a colourful life. In 1980, he became the lawyer for the far-right Liberty Lobby, the publisher of *The Spotlight* newspaper. Liberty Lobby's founder Willis Carto had quit the John Birch Society in 1958 because its anti-communism was insufficiently antisemitic, and set up various groups, including the Institute for Historical Review, a respectable-sounding home for Holocaust denial. Lane himself launched an anti-Israel newsletter, *Zionist Watch*. He also represented James Earl Ray, the white nationalist assassin of Martin Luther King, in the belief that he was a patsy in a government plot. Another client was the People's Temple cult led by Jim Jones, which Lane insisted was the victim of a 'massive conspiracy' by the CIA and FBI. Lane was present in Jonestown, Guyana, when 918 people died by murder or suicide under Jones's orders. But his questionable judgement did not slow him down. In 2011, at the age of 84, he published *Last Word: My Indictment of the CIA in the Murder of JFK*.

Garrison, Marrs and Lane demonstrated how easily an event conspiracy theory could morph into a grand systemic conspiracy theory. In *JFK*'s greatest set piece, the government informant known as X, played by Donald Sutherland, informs Garrison that Kennedy's murder is just a single component in one big plot extending from 'black ops' against communists in post-war Europe to Cuba and Vietnam. If Kennedy had lived, the argument goes, he would have de-escalated the conflict in Vietnam, broken up the CIA and ended the Cold War.

'Who benefited?' asks X. *Cui bono?* One answer was Lyndon Johnson, who became president after Kennedy's death. Another was America's defence and security establishment, which wanted to retain the money and power it derived from the Cold War.

It is not hard to see why Stone liked X's explanation. It is a historical fact that the crucial justification for escalating the Vietnam War, the North Vietnamese attack on US ships in the Gulf of Tonkin on 4 August 1964, never actually happened and the Johnson administration lied. Stone's personal formative trauma was the 14 months he spent fighting in Vietnam and seeing his friends die. He went on to make three movies about the war. The way X tells it, everything that Stone experienced and witnessed there – the whole damn war – could have been avoided if only Kennedy had lived. Hence Stone himself was a victim of the plot he described.

As Costner's Garrison says in the movie: 'The ghost of John F. Kennedy confronts us with the secret murder at the heart of the American dream.' Stone had a sentimental view of Kennedy as a thwarted pacifist, even though the president was already sending troops to Vietnam and most historians agree that he would have continued to do so. But if Kennedy's death was the moment it all went wrong for America, then the victim must be a martyred saint and the killers who stole the future must be pure evil.

Stone had his own version of the Illuminati, the Hidden Hand or Them. It was called 'the Beast' – a word straight from the Book of Revelation. In a 1996 interview, he threaded the beads of the assassinations of JFK, Robert Kennedy and Martin Luther King and the downfall of Richard Nixon: 'These four men came from different political perspectives, but they were pushing the envelope, trying to lead America to new levels,' he said. 'We posit that, in some way, they pissed off what we call "the Beast", the Beast being a force, or forces, greater than the presidency.' X's speech in the film unveiled the Beast.

On first viewing, Sutherland's bravura 17-minute mono-logue, bolstered by documentary-style footage, is irresistibly persuasive. But it is fiction dressed as fact. The speech was largely taken from a 1967 bestseller, *The Report from Iron Mountain on the Possibility and Desirability of Peace*. Introduced by the journalist Leonard Lewin, the book purported to be the leaked findings of a 15-member Special Study Group, exploring the dire consequences of world peace for the US government. 'The organization of a society for the possibility of war is its principal political stabilizer,' it argued. The report's veracity was questioned by journalists and hotly denied by the government, and rightly so. In 1972, Lewin admitted that he had written it himself, as a vicious parody of defence think-tanks. It was a brilliant hoax.

In 1990, however, the book was reprinted by the Holocaust-denying Liberty Lobby, apparently in the belief that it was real. Lewin, who was a Jewish liberal, was horrified and successfully sued to block its publication. The man who had brought it to Liberty Lobby was L. Fletcher Prouty, a former US Air Force colonel who had worked at the Pentagon under Eisenhower and Kennedy. In his 1973 book *The Secret Team: The CIA and Its Allies in Control of the United States and the World*, Prouty claimed that a secret 'power elite' ran the world and that the assassination was a *coup d'état* to replace Kennedy with their puppet Johnson.

Prouty was the real X. He gave *Report from Iron Mountain* to Stone, who hired him as a consultant on the movie. When Prouty's links to Liberty Lobby were exposed, Stone not only defended him but went so far as to write the introduction to his JFK book, claiming that Lewin's spoof was 'based on' a real study. So the heart of *JFK*'s left-wing systemic conspiracy theory was a prank narrated by a far-right crank.

Media attacks on *JFK* began when a draft screenplay was leaked months before its release, and grew so intense that Stone became highly defensive. He hotly claimed that it was 'not a true story per se' but an experiment in 'exploring all possible scenarios of who killed Kennedy and why'. He compared his project to Shakespeare creatively rewriting history in *Henry V*. But this was disingenuous. As viewers, we are obviously meant to believe that Garrison is on the right track, otherwise why are we watching a three-hour movie about him? The average audience member has no way of knowing which scenes are accurate, which are speculative and which are entirely imagined. Stone contradicted himself when he admitted that he was far from neutral: 'My own conclusions go harder and further than the film.' Almost every article that disparaged *JFK*'s veracity provoked a furiously detailed letter from the director. So much for the *Henry V* defence.

Despite three decades of criticism, Stone has never backed down. 'There's nothing in the movie that I would go back on,' he said in 2013. In fact, on its thirtieth anniversary he released a documentary, *JFK Revisited: Through the Looking Glass*, in which he said bluntly: 'Conspiracy theory has become conspiracy fact.' But the film recycled the same old arguments.

'Don't take my word for it, don't believe me,' X tells Garrison. 'Do your own work, your own thinking.' But for millions of viewers, the impact of *JFK* could be summed up by Garrison's line: 'My eyes have opened, and once they're open, believe me, what used to look normal seems insane.' By extension, what seems insane could be the truth. 'I always thought Oswald was just a nut and another nut shot him,' one college student told *New York Newsday* after seeing the movie. 'That's basically what I was taught. But now I'm convinced it was a plot.' Bill Alexander, a former Dallas assistant DA, complained that the sheer number of books and films about the assassination convinced people there had been a conspiracy. The veracity of these stories mattered less than their volume: 'It seems like there is so much written about it, they figure some of it must be right.' If there's enough smoke, there must be a fire.

Stephen E. Ambrose concluded that the movie's success 'may tell us more about the attitude people have toward their government and their educational experiences than it does about the Kennedy assassination. They believe that government is a conspiracy and that the history they were taught in school is all lie and myth . . . It is because people are so often lied to by their governments that they say, "I wouldn't put anything past those guys" and mean it.'

Still, the fact remains that more than 60 years after the assassination and 30 years after *JFK* inspired the creation of the Assassination Records Review Board, there have been no decisive revelations, incriminating leaks or deathbed confessions to wrap things up once and for all. JFK researchers are still where they were in 1966: capable of casting enormous doubt on the Warren Commission's flawed account but unable to replace it with a solid, coherent narrative of their own.

A much better fictional account of the assassination is Don DeLillo's 1988 novel *Libra*. 'There is enough mystery in the facts as we know them, enough of conspiracy, coincidence, loose ends, dead ends, multiple interpretations,' one character concludes. 'There is no need . . . to invent the grand and masterful scheme, the plot that reaches flawlessly in a dozen directions.' In the following decade, however, the craving for a giant conspiracy would grow larger than ever.

CHAPTER FOUR
The Mainstreaming of Conspiracy Theories

America in the 1990s had a doppelgänger. On the face of it, this was a period of security and prosperity, with liberal democracy emerging triumphant from the Cold War. But there was a shadow self, which seemed to bear no connection to the first: a decade of cults, plots, bombs, mass shootings, pre-millennium tension and lethal paranoia. Conspiracy theorists who had previously relied on books, pamphlets and meetings to spread the word were able to form an international network via the new World Wide Web. The paranoid style bloomed around the world, but nowhere more strikingly than in the US.

The bridge between these parallel 1990s was the First Couple: Bill and Hillary Clinton. In one version of reality they were the smiling faces of slick, technocratic centrism. In the other they were the dark stars of an unfathomably evil criminal conspiracy.

On 20 July 1993, Vince Foster, President Clinton's deputy White House counsel, was found dead in Fort Marcy Park, just outside Washington DC. His right hand was still clutching a Colt .38 special. His briefcase contained a draft resignation letter, torn into 27 pieces, which described his deep unhappiness and hatred of Washington life. Foster had been receiving treatment for depression. An autopsy concluded that he had shot himself in the mouth, a verdict that was later confirmed by five separate official investigations, three of which were overseen by the president's Republican opponents. But the Clintons' enemies told a different story.

During the 1992 election campaign, rumours had swirled around Bill Clinton's tenure as governor of Arkansas. There were claims of multiple affairs, some of which turned out to be true. There was also a financial entanglement involving the failure of the Whitewater Development Corporation. But these old-fashioned political scandals of sex and money were just the skeleton for an ever-growing conspiracy theory that painted the Clintons as a ruthless criminal gang, knocking off anyone who knew too much. Foster's tragic death kicked this narrative into overdrive.

In 1993, the conservative billionaire Richard Mellon Scaife funded the blandly named Editorial Improvement Project, nicknamed the Arkansas Project, hiring professional and amateur investigators to dig up dirt on the Clintons. Whitewater and adultery were just the start. The project also tried to tie the couple to murder and drug-smuggling. One of Scaife's pet reporters, Christopher W. Ruddy, published a book called *The Strange Death of Vince Foster*, using inconsistencies and errors in the police investigation to imply that the Clintons had ordered the lawyer's murder. The documentary *The Clinton Chronicles* was a cult smash. Roger Stone, a veteran Republican operative who had begun his political career doing dirty tricks for the Nixon campaign, coined the phrase 'Clinton body count'. Nixon himself told an aide that the 'Foster suicide smells to high heaven'.

In 1997, a White House document observed how

'right-wing activists feed conspiracy theories and innuendo from the fringes into the mainstream media': online activists planted stories in sympathetic conservative publications, who gave them enough legitimacy to be picked up by the rest of the press, which then disseminated them even as it questioned their veracity. And it was not just happening in the US. In the UK, Ambrose Evans-Pritchard of the *Sunday Telegraph* gave the Vince Foster theories a veneer of establishment credibility. In 1998, Hillary Clinton famously described this disinformation pipeline as a 'vast right-wing conspiracy'.

Clinton was trying to discredit the entirely true allegations that her husband had had an affair with a junior White House aide called Monica Lewinsky, but she was not wrong about the smear network. One Arkansas Project reporter, David Brock, later repudiated his work and exposed the project, calling himself 'a witting cog in the Republican sleaze machine'. Conservatives obviously did not like losing the White House to a Democrat. They especially did not like a liberal, baby-boomer president who allowed gays into the military and used to smoke weed. And they *really* did not like a first lady who was a pro-choice feminist with ideas of her own. So they made things up.

Conservative evangelical pastors like Jerry Falwell wove anti-Clinton conspiracy theories into their sermons. Right-wing talk-radio hosts like Rush Limbaugh broadcast them to millions. Internet chatrooms buzzed with them. The Lewinsky scandal, which consumed much of Bill Clinton's second term, gave the rumours credibility even though Ken Starr, the fanatically anti-Clinton lawyer who investigated the couple for four years, found no evidence for most of them, including the alleged murder of Vince Foster.

All powerful politicians come under attack. That is part

of the job. But the anti-Clinton effort weaponised conspiracy theories like never before, with dangerous consequences. In the normal democratic process, competing factions consider their opponents incompetent or wrong and try to present a better offer. But in this new narrative, the Clintons were completely immoral, evil, even satanic. There was no crime they wouldn't consider, no lie they wouldn't tell. The Revelation-inspired absolutism of conspiracy theory had boiled over into day-to-day political life. Clinton hysteria injected it into the bloodstream of the conservative movement to a degree the John Birch Society only dreamed of. It marked the beginning of the Republican Party's long radicalisation into a doomsday cult led by the reality-mangling Donald Trump.

President Clinton also had to deal with a much more violent kind of conspiracism. The survivalist militia movement had sprung out of the economic and political crises of the 1970s. Intense men stockpiled guns and supplies in preparation for the collapse of civilisation and its Mad Max aftermath – a possibility that they seemed to crave more than they feared. During the 1980s, the movement became entangled with far-right terrorism. In 1985, the Oregon-based militia Posse Comitatus claimed: 'Our nation is now completely under the control of the International Invisible government of the World Jewry.' The militias called this the Zionist Occupation Government (ZOG).

The militia's set text was *The Turner Diaries*, a lurid 1978 novel that has been implicated in bank robberies, murders and bomb plots around the world. Written by a neo-Nazi, William Luther Pierce, the novel describes how a white nationalist group, the 'Organization', violently overthrows the Jewish-led 'System', leading to civil war, nuclear strikes on New York,

Israel and the Soviet Union, and genocidal world conquest. 'The dream of a white world,' it concludes, 'finally became a certainty.' By the 1990s, the militias' nemesis was not just communism or Zionism but the US state itself. 'Anyone who talks about communism doesn't get it any more,' said one militia member. 'The enemy is fascism in the White House.'

Two law enforcement disasters gave the militia movement martyrs and villains. In August 1992, agents from the Federal Bureau of Alcohol, Tobacco and Firearms (ATF) showed up at a cabin on Ruby Ridge, Idaho, to arrest Randy Weaver, a white supremacist. The operation went badly wrong, leaving Weaver's wife and 14-year-old son dead. Eight months later, in Waco, Texas, agents of the ATF and the FBI laid siege to the compound of the Branch Davidians, an apocalyptic sect led by the self-proclaimed Messiah David Koresh. The siege ended on 19 April, six days into Weaver's trial, with the compound in flames and 76 Branch Davidians dead, including Koresh. Like the Weavers, they were victims of both their own paranoia and the government's. The federal agents thought they were far more dangerous than they actually were.

The militias saw in these showdowns confirmation of their suspicion that the state wanted to murder them. One of the militias radicalised by Ruby Ridge and Waco kept an ever-growing dossier of evidence, based on the John Birch Society's *Blue Book*, which used 'the enemy's own words' to prove the conspiracy. It included a speech made by President George H. W. Bush on 11 September 1990. He had made the unfortunate decision to call his vision of a post-Cold War era of peace, prosperity and international cooperation 'a new world order'. There was nothing unusual about that – the phrase had been used in similar contexts by Winston Churchill, Woodrow Wilson and H. G. Wells. But in 1971,

Gary Allen's *None Dare Call It Conspiracy* had popularised it as a synonym for one-world government. As a member of the Trilateral Commission and the Council of Foreign Relations, the former head of the CIA *and* an oil tycoon, Bush could not have set off more flashing red lights for conspiracy theorists.

The New World Order became the consensus name for the one-big-plot conspiracy theory. A sign on Randy Weaver's cabin at Ruby Ridge, for example, read: *STOP THE NEW WORLD ORDER*. The Anti-Defamation League, a Jewish advocacy group, claimed that it was a euphemism for the international Jewish conspiracy, but for believers it was much bigger than that – it was satanic. 'The Book of Revelation speaks of a one-world order, one financial order, a one-world religion,' explained one of them, paraphrasing somewhat.

The New World Order developed a complex mythology involving some combination of the following: a United Nations-led military invasion of the USA, black helicopters, the confiscation of firearms, microchip-enabled mind control, Federal Emergency Management Agency (FEMA) concentration camps for 'patriots' and a network of secret societies orchestrating all of the above via traitors in the US government.

During the 1980s, previously separate subcultures – ufology, far-right militias, the New Age community – converged around this spectre of the New World Order. Milton William Cooper's *Behold a Pale Horse* pulled together the New World Order, the Book of Revelation, the Illuminati, the Freemasons, the Knights Templar, the Jesuits, the Nazis, the Rothschilds, the Bilderberg group, the Trilateral Commission, the *Protocols of the Elders of Zion*, *Alternative 3*, the Kennedy assassination and AIDS into the superconspiracy theory of a plot by malevolent extraterrestrials. 'We have been taught lies,' Cooper wrote. 'Reality is not at all what we perceive it to be.' It was Cooper who popularised the now-ubiquitous insult 'sheeple' to describe docile, gullible citizens. *Behold a Pale Horse* went straight onto the militias' core reading list, alongside *The Turner Diaries*, Pat Robertson's *The New World Order* and, to the author's dismay, Leonard Lewin's misunderstood parody *Report from Iron Mountain*.

The intellectual lineage, if intellectual is indeed the right word, was clear. Cooper drew on 200 years of Illuminati-related conspiracy theories, going back through Gary Allen, Robert Welch, William Carr, Gerald Winrod and Nesta Webster, all the way to John Robison and August Barruel. Each writer added new ingredients to the mix until the imagined plot was so impossibly vast and intricate that it made Robison and Barruel look like level-headed fellows with some legitimate questions about the French Revolution.

One person who wanted to avenge the victims of Ruby Ridge and Waco was Timothy McVeigh, a 27-year-old decorated Gulf War veteran. He was a pro-gun survivalist who had driven to Waco during the siege to show his support and told a reporter: 'I believe we are slowly turning into a socialist government . . . and the people need to prepare to defend themselves against government control.' He had also made pilgrimages to Randy Weaver's cabin and the alleged UFO hotspot Area 51.

On the morning of 19 April 1995, the second anniversary of the Waco fire, McVeigh parked a huge truck-mounted bomb outside the Alfred P. Murrah Federal Building in Oklahoma City, which he believed was the local headquarters of the New World Order. He wanted to light the fuse for a revolution. At 9.02 a.m., the bomb detonated, killing 168 people, including 19 children in the building's daycare centre. Until 9/11, it was the most lethal terrorist attack ever to take place on American soil. The police who searched McVeigh's car found pages from *The Turner Diaries*. But McVeigh's fellow conspiracy theorists, with depressing predictability, redefined the bombing as another event conspiracy theory, with McVeigh the innocent patsy.

'False flag' is an old naval term for pirate ships that used friendly banners so that they could safely approach vessels before unrolling the Jolly Roger flag. During the 1980s, it acquired a broader meaning. According to the *Oxford English Dictionary*, a false flag is 'an event or action (typically political or military in nature) secretly orchestrated by someone other than the person or organization that appears to be responsible for it'. The purpose is to frame your enemies as a pretext for war or repressive legislation. The Reichstag fire was an alleged false flag. The shelling of the Russian village of Mainila, which justified the Soviet invasion of Finland in 1939, was a real false flag. The militia movement claimed that Oklahoma City was a false flag.

An atrocity motivated by conspiracy theories thus became the inspiration for more. Milton William Cooper combined two classic conspiracy theories by calling McVeigh 'the Lee Harvey Oswald of the American Reichstag'. The more respectable novelist Gore Vidal insinuated in *Vanity Fair* that McVeigh 'neither made nor set off the bomb outside the Murrah building' and that the bombing was 'pseudo terrorism, perpetrated by compartmentalized covert operators for the purposes of state police power'. Annoyingly for both of them, McVeigh repeatedly confessed to acting alone and neatly summed up the emotional appeal of imagining that he hadn't: 'Isn't it kind of scary that one man could wreak this kind of hell?'

Oklahoma City was a wake-up call that made the New

World Order theory a cause for concern rather than amusement. Shortly after the bombing, the journalist Michael Kelly coined the term 'fusion paranoia' to describe the power of conspiracy theories to bring together people from the left and the right. The pioneer of this strange alliance was Lyndon LaRouche, a businessman, a serial presidential candidate and the most energetic American conspiracy theorist of the late twentieth century. Broadly speaking, LaRouche started out on the Trotskyist hard left and migrated towards the far right, but in the 1990s he attacked mainstream Democrats from both the right (climate change denial) and the left (universal healthcare), which made him hard to pin down.

Kelly observed that millions of Americans had been absorbed into the paranoid style despite their political differences, with old hippies and Holocaust deniers alike united against the evil ruling elites. They converged on key images, such as implanted microchips or black helicopters, and on one fundamental idea: 'Although fusion paranoia draws from, and plays to, the left and the right, it rejects that bipolar model for a more primal polarity: Us versus Them.'

During the 1990s, conspiracy theories entered the mainstream more than ever. The *OED* didn't add a definition for *conspiracy theory* until 1997. Pat Buchanan, who came second in the Republican primaries in 1996 with attacks on the New World Order, was a conspiracy theorist. So, less obviously, was Ross Perot, the eccentric businessman who won 19 per cent of the vote in 1992 and 8 per cent in 1996, making him one of the most successful third-party candidates in US history. 'Beliefs once consigned to the outermost fringes of American political and religious life now seem less isolated and stigmatizing than they once did,' wrote Michael Barkun in 1996.

By coincidence (or was it?!) the end of the millennium coincided with the end of communism as a global force. One theory is that the collapse of the Soviet Union demolished the Us versus Them binary of the Cold War and created a demand for substitutes. Another theory is that people were simply bored and restless in what the political scientist Francis Fukuyama called 'the end of history': the triumph of liberal capitalist democracy. 'The end of history will be a very sad time,' Fukuyama wrote in 1989. He predicted that people would mourn the replacement of dramatic ideological struggle with bland consumerism and technocratic problem-solving. 'Perhaps the very prospect of centuries of boredom at the end of history will serve to get history started once again.' Conspiracy theories were one way to make life interesting again.

Increasingly it seemed as if nothing dramatic could happen without inspiring conspiracy theories: the foiled World Trade Center bombing in 1993, the crashing of TWA Flight 800 in 1996, the death of Princess Diana in 1997. Shortly after the murder of rapper Tupac Shakur in 1996, the title of his first posthumous album seemed to endorse rumours that all was not as it seemed: *The Don Killuminati: The 7 Day Theory*. A 1996 US Air Force report on weather modification spawned a hugely popular theory that the condensation trails left by aircraft were 'chemtrails', containing chemical or biological agents, for purposes such as mind or population control. America's most popular late-night radio show was Art Bell's *Coast to Coast AM*, where no conspiracy theory was out of bounds.

The Shakespeare scholar James Shapiro observed that the old argument about whether the real author of Shakespeare's plays was the Earl of Oxford became dramatically more popular during the 1990s – less as an academic debate than as another conspiracy theory to add to the pile. 'In such a climate, a minor act of conspiratorial suppression on the part of Tudor authorities made perfect sense – and in comparison, was small beer,' he wrote.

The most popular mainstream vessel for conspiracy theories was *The X-Files*, which ran on Fox between 1993 and 2002 and attracted as many as 20 million viewers a week. Chris Carter's show was mercifully more Area 51 than the *Protocols of the Elders of Zion*. Fox Mulder (played by David Duchovny) and Dana Scully (played by Gillian Anderson) investigate paranormal cases for the FBI, with occasional assistance from some nerdy 'independent researchers' calling themselves the Lone Gunmen. Carter initially envisaged an ongoing argument about the nature of reality between the chronically suspicious Mulder and the more cool-headed Scully, but he soon found that the show was only compelling if Mulder was always right: there *was* more than met the eye. The cards were stacked in favour of paranoia.

Mulder and Scully gradually discover that a powerful group called the Syndicate is secretly collaborating with an alien race that wants to colonise the earth – a story similar to the one in *Behold a Pale Horse*. The Cigarette-Smoking Man (played by William B. Davis), a shadowy Syndicate operative complicit in everything from the JFK assassination to the Roswell incident, is the nicotine-stained embodiment of the Hidden Hand, aka the Beast.

Most viewers saw *The X-Files* as just spooky fun, but conspiracy theorists perceived it as a dramatised endorsement of what they already suspected. Mulder's credo summed up the show's appeal: 'I want to believe.' A 1997 CNN/*Time* poll found that '80 percent of Americans think the government is hiding knowledge of the existence of extraterrestrial lifeforms'. Carter insisted that while he would love to find evidence of UFOs, his show was meant to be fiction: 'If – and it's a big if – anyone does believe it is true, that merely suggests we are reflecting something wider in society.'

He was right about that. Conspiracy theories were so popular that in 1997, Mel Gibson starred in a film called simply *Conspiracy Theory*. Gibson plays a paranoiac who appears to be delusional, but the twist is that he is right: the black helicopters descend. 'What if your most paranoid nightmares had just come true?' asks the tagline. The movie is both a parody and a validation of conspiracy theories. Other nineties movies suggested that the world was not as it seemed: *The Matrix*, *The Truman Show*, *Fight Club*. Popular culture was telling us to look closer. In *The Matrix*, Morpheus (played by Laurence Fishburne) offers Neo (played by Keanu Reeves) a choice of two pills: 'After this, there is no turning back. You take the blue pill – the story ends, you wake up in your bed and believe whatever you want to believe. You take the red pill – you stay in Wonderland and I show you how deep the rabbit hole goes.' Both the rabbit hole and the red pill became shorthand for conspiracy theories and are still in constant use today.

For people who saw truth in these high-concept entertainments, reality itself was a conspiracy. As Naomi Klein wrote in *Doppelganger*: 'We are not having disagreements about differing interpretations of reality – we are having disagreements about who is in reality and who is in a simulation.'

On 11 September 2001, two passenger jets flew into New York's World Trade Center and a third crashed into the Pentagon. At this point, for an event of this magnitude, conspiracy theories were inevitable. Here was a world-changing catastrophe, thought to be impossible, that led to assaults on civil liberties and wars that neoconservatives in the administration of George W. Bush wanted anyway.

According to the official narrative, 9/11 was indeed a conspiracy, planned by an international network and executed by a small group of fanatics to achieve a political goal. Al-Qaeda's Osama bin Laden proudly took responsibility for it. But that was the wrong kind of conspiracy – too obvious, too boring, too much in line with Bush's political agenda.

Alternative theories began to proliferate while the wreckage was still smouldering and bodies were being pulled from the rubble. 'There was a sense of disbelief that a man in a cave in Afghanistan could reach out and humiliate the most powerful nation in the history of the world,' explained Lawrence Wright, author of *The Looming Tower*, a prize-winning book about 9/11. 'How could that happen? It must be that something else was at work and because we are so powerful, we must have done it to ourselves.'

The mildest variant was that the Bush administration knew in advance about the attacks and let them happen. In a 2004 Zogby poll, nearly two thirds of New Yorkers under 30 believed that Bush had ignored crucial intelligence. The Let It Happen on Purpose (LIHOP) theory was a descendant of the revisionist allegation, first promoted by Republican isolationists, that President Franklin D. Roosevelt knew in advance about the attack on Pearl Harbor in December 1941 and did nothing because he wanted an excuse to join the war. 'A gift from the gods had been put into Roosevelt's hands,' claimed John T. Flynn in *The Truth About Pearl Harbor*. As usual, it falls apart upon the merest examination. For one thing, Roosevelt wanted war with Germany, not Japan. It was Hitler who declared war on the USA. If he had not, Roosevelt would have been locked in combat with the enemy he didn't want. And yet the story persisted.

The second 9/11 theory was that the Bush administration had Made It Happen on Purpose (MIHOP): a false-flag attack on a mind-boggling scale. Conspiracy theorists moulded a handful of apparent anomalies into outrageous claims. They said that the US Air Force should have been able to intercept the hijacked planes before they reached New York. They said that the collapse of the Twin Towers and WTC7, a smaller building nearby that was not directly hit, could not have been caused by the planes, only by controlled demolition – a belief popularised by the phrase 'jet fuel can't melt steel beams'. They said that the Pentagon was hit by a missile, not American Airlines Flight 77. And they said that United Airlines Flight 93 was not in fact brought down by brave passengers before it could reach Washington DC but landed safely, where its passengers were mysteriously disposed of. Their desperate last-minute phone calls to loved ones had all been faked.

Unsurprisingly, there was an antisemitic wrinkle involving Israeli intelligence. A Syrian government newspaper started a rumour that 4,000 Jewish employees at the World Trade Center had been warned not to show up to work that day, even though at least 10 per cent of the actual victims were Jewish. 'Who told 4,000 Israeli workers at the Twin Towers to stay home that day?' asked the poet Amiri Baraka in a poem that related 9/11 to everything from slavery to the death of Princess Diana. It was a complete fabrication. A related theory claimed that the buildings' new owner, the Jewish businessman Larry Silverstein, had demolished them for the insurance money. In 2008, 43 per cent of Egyptians in a World Public Opinion poll blamed Israel for 9/11.

The 9/11 sceptics called themselves 'truthers'. They were

the descendants of the JFK researchers, and in some cases the same people. 'Scratch the surface of a middle-aged 9/11 truther and you are almost guaranteed to find a JFK conspiracist,' wrote the journalist Jonathan Kay. The reports of the 9/11 Commission and the National Institute of Standards and Technology were their equivalents of the Warren Report. As long as President Bush remained popular, 9/11 conspiracy theories were only successful outside the US. Thierry Meyssan's *9/11: The Big Lie* topped France's bestseller chart for six weeks in spring 2002, with no US equivalent. But the more distrusted Bush became, the more the theories flourished on home turf.

Part of the reason for this distrust was that even as the US government was angrily rebutting conspiracy theories about 9/11, it was busily building conspiracy theories of its own about Iraq's Saddam Hussein. Neoconservatives in the Bush administration had been hoping to remove Saddam since the first Gulf War in 1991, and a decade later they finally got their chance.

It was no longer enough to say that Saddam was a genocidal, quasi-fascist dictator and serial warmonger. After all, during the Cold War, the US had installed more dictators than it had removed. So the *casus belli* rested on two more urgent claims. First, Bush insisted that Saddam had been complicit in 9/11. This was despite the fact that his secular nationalist regime was extremely hostile to Islamists and had no proven ties to al-Qaeda. When this argument proved unpersuasive, the president proposed another: Saddam was developing weapons of mass destruction (WMDs) to use on the West. This was the case that convinced the US and UK public and around 40 international allies to support the invasion of Iraq without a United Nations mandate. Nine in ten Americans told Gallup that they expected the invasion force to find evidence of WMDs or a project to develop them. But after the US-led coalition invaded Iraq in March 2003, it soon emerged that there was no sign whatsoever of WMDs. The case for war had been built on at best a delusion and at worst an outright lie.

The Iraq War proved that governments of major powers can be susceptible to conspiracy theories, but it also demonstrated the difference between them and full-time conspiracy theorists. When no evidence of WMDs was found, Bush maintained that he had genuinely believed otherwise. He did not double down and claim that the weapons had been hidden as part of the plot. He reluctantly bowed to reality. This should have dampened the conspiracy theories. After all, a president mendacious enough to stage the destruction of the Twin Towers would probably have taken the time to plant incriminating evidence rather than allow himself to be shown to have taken his country to war on a false pretext. But the theories continued unabated.

Bush's deceit about WMDs, and Iraq's subsequent descent into chaos, unleashed the truthers. The dam broke with *The New Pearl Harbor*, a 2004 book by a philosophy professor in California, David Ray Griffin, and *Loose Change*, a 2005 viral documentary directed by 21-year-old Dylan Avery. *Loose Change* was a classic example of conspiracist storytelling, mixing genuine inconsistencies, slick editing and a calm, authoritative voiceover with unreliable sources, cherry-picked data and sly insinuations. 'It was just so easy to believe anything terrible about your government because you were seeing all of these terrible things,' Avery said later.

Loose Change made hay with Operation Northwoods, a shocking 1962 Pentagon proposal to stage terrorist attacks on American soil and pin them on communist Cuba as an excuse for military action. President Kennedy nixed this monstrous idea, but its existence proved that false flags had been officially considered at least once. (One theory held that Kennedy had been murdered precisely because he had vetoed Northwoods.) *Loose Change* also used the enemy's own words. In a 2000 report for the neoconservative Project for the New American Century, Defense Secretary Donald Rumsfeld had written: 'The process of [military] transformation, even if it brings revolutionary change, is likely to be a long one, absent some catastrophic and catalyzing event – like a new Pearl Harbor.' Avery's movie implied that Rumsfeld had organised exactly that. It omitted the rather problematic fact that he would have been ordering a terrorist strike on the Pentagon when he was personally inside the building.

Curiously, *Loose Change* came out shortly after the magazine *Popular Mechanics* had published a 5,500-word point-by-point debunking of 9/11 conspiracy theories, carefully explaining why the buildings collapsed as they did. It turned out, for instance, that while jet fuel could not melt steel beams, it could weaken them sufficiently for the buildings to give way. It was too late, however. There was no putting the genie back in the bottle. 'This is a self-confirming hypothesis for the people who hold it,' said *Popular Mechanics* editor James Meigs. 'In that sense it is immune from any kind of refutation and it is very similar to . . . a really hardcore, doctrinaire Marxist or a hardcore fundamentalist creationist. They have sort of a divine answer to every argument you might make.' The magazine's subsequent book, *Debunking 9/11 Myths*, prompted a truther response ludicrously entitled *Debunking 9/11 Debunking*.

The *Guardian* journalist George Monbiot summed up the absurdity of the truther case: '[The conspiracy] could not have been executed without the help of demolition experts, the security firms guarding the World Trade Center, Mayor Giuliani . . . much of the US Air Force, the Federal Aviation Administration and the North American Aerospace Defense Command, the relatives of the people "killed" in the plane crashes, the rest of the Pentagon's staff, the Los Alamos laboratories, the FBI, the CIA and the investigators who picked through the rubble.' This immensely complicated government scheme to murder thousands of US citizens with the aid of hundreds of tight-lipped accomplices was somehow meant to be more credible than the official story. But the theory's implausibility made little difference. By the fifth anniversary of the attacks, one in three Americans said that the Bush administration had either orchestrated or permitted the attacks to justify war in the Middle East. As Monbiot wrote: 'People believe *Loose Change* because it proposes a closed world: comprehensible, controllable, small. Despite the great evil which runs it, it is more companionable than the chaos which really governs our lives, a world without destination or purpose.'

The 9/11 Truth Movement attracted current or former politicians, officials and celebrities from around the world, but its most powerful ally was the internet. The first version of *Loose Change* was released just two months after the debut of a brand-new platform called YouTube. Within a year it had received tens of millions of views. With the advent of video streaming, social media and smartphones, conspiracy theories could fly around the world like never before. The YouTube algorithm proved to be an amazingly efficient radicalisation tool, pushing users down rabbit holes of paranoia rather than promoting a range of narratives.

Gradually, *Loose Change* director Dylan Avery distanced himself from the truther movement he had helped to build, because, he said, it had been taken over by full-time conspiracy theorists. 'I was afraid I was becoming one of them – someone who sees conspiracy around every corner,' he said. 'Before, when you said you believed in 9/11 Truth, it meant the original investigation was shoddy. But you weren't a nut-job. Now, as soon as something happens, people say it's a false flag.'

In his 1997 book *Conspiracy*, Daniel Pipes was remarkably optimistic about the future of conspiracy theories. He thought that 'serious conspiracism' in the West 'belongs more to the past than the future. It no longer drives the actions of governments or other major institutions.' As democracies matured, Pipes argued, they became less susceptible to paranoid leaders. Even in Russia, 'the pervasive conspiracism of earlier times appears to be in retreat'. He could not have been more wrong.

Something changed after 9/11. Prior to that, it was still possible to regard conspiracy theorists as entertaining kooks who weren't doing any real harm. The darker history of conspiracy theories – their role in justifying tyranny, terrorism and genocide – was well documented but not keenly felt. The ideas promoted in *The X-Files* were over here and the ideas that killed 168 people in Oklahoma City were over there.

One person who realised that he had missed the big picture was the journalist Jon Ronson. In April 2001, he published *Them: Adventures with Extremists*, a playful series of encounters with paranoid characters including Randy Weaver's daughter Rachel, the Grand Wizard of the Ku Klux Klan, a British jihadi, David Icke, and Alex Jones of InfoWars. These seemingly disparate people were united by their belief in the 'secret rulers of the world', although the cabal's alleged membership changed from person to person.

Ronson had been collecting references to the Bilderberg group, an annual gathering of influential people named after the site of the first meeting in 1954: the Bilderberg Hotel in Oosterbeek, Netherlands. People we have already met, like Phyllis Schlafly and Gary Allen, suggested that the forum was the nerve centre of the one-world conspiracy. The neo-Nazi who planted three nail bombs in London in 1999 claimed that the Bilderbergers controlled prime minister Tony Blair. The Serbian leader Slobodan Milošević blamed the Bilderbergers for fomenting war in the former Yugoslavia. 'It's a pyramid,' Alex Jones explained to Ronson. 'They're way up there. Below them you've got the IMF, the World Bank, the United Nations, then you've got us down here, the cattle, the human resources.'

Ronson invited the reader to chuckle at these creepy but fundamentally irrelevant outliers. In the paperback edition, though, he acknowledged that the book was 'a snapshot of life in the Western world on 10 September 2001' and that it read completely differently now. Ronson saw that al-Qaeda and the truthers were two sides of the same coin: they both believed in 'an internationalist Western conspiracy conducted by a tiny, secretive elite, whose ultimate aim is to destroy all opposition, implement a planetary takeover, and establish themselves as a World Government'. The people he had been meeting were not marginal crackpots at all. They were the future.

CHAPTER FIVE
The Conspiracy Industry

In 2021, *The X-Files* creator Chris Carter confessed some regrets. 'Do I believe the government lies to us?' he wrote in the *New York Times*. 'Absolutely. I'm a child of Watergate. Do I believe in conspiracies? Certainly.' But, he clarified, he was not a conspiracy theorist and he now worried that his TV show had played a role in America's epistemological collapse: '"The Truth Is Out There", "Trust No One", "Deny Everything" went the provocative catchphrases on *The X-Files*, but that was in the '90s, when we had a relatively shared reality. The slogans are now a fact of life.'

The X-Files had caught the imagination during a period when, despite Timothy McVeigh and the Arkansas Project, conspiracy theories were widely considered the titillatingly exotic habit of a wacky minority. By 2021, however, conspiracism had become a widespread psychological addiction, a political strategy and a booming market. Conspiracy theories may have been around for a very long time, but the establishment of what is in effect a paranoia industry is relatively recent, with dire consequences for democracy.

As a result, the term 'conspiracy theorist' became too broad to explain the sheer diversity of motives and behaviours on offer. The classic conspiracy researcher, who diligently pored over the Warren Report but was embarrassed by far-fetched allegations of global plots, suddenly seemed sweetly old-fashioned. The conspiracy hobbyist, who enjoyed mysteries, games and eccentric counter-knowledge, appeared almost charming.

In their place were new breeds of conspiracist, who were far more dangerous and required more explanation: the conspiracy addict, the conspiracy entrepreneur, the conspiracy leader and the conspiracy cult.

The conspiracy addict

Naomi Wolf's 1990 book *The Beauty Myth* was described as the most important feminist book since the 1970s Second Wave and made its author a superstar intellectual. Young, eloquent and inspiring, Wolf seemed to embody the hopes of a feminist revival in the 1990s. She was a staunch Democrat who went on to consult on Bill Clinton's re-election campaign in 1996 and Al Gore's presidential bid in 2000.

During the George W. Bush years, Wolf became more politically flamboyant. Her 2007 book *The End of America: Letter of Warning to a Patriot* argued that Bush was taking America to the brink of fascism. Though hyperbolic, this language was not unusual on the left. But as her celebrity waned, her dabble in conspiracy theories turned into a headlong dive. In 2013–14 alone, she doubted the official narrative about everything from NSA whistleblower Edward Snowden and the ISIS beheadings of Western captives to the West African Ebola outbreak and the Scottish independence referendum. Wolf had become a conspiracy addict – somebody who automatically assumes a plot behind every shocking event, slotting the latest news into a prefabricated template. *Nothing* is as it seems.

Despite this bizarre turn, she maintained a mainstream career until, in 2019, she lived every scholar's nightmare. During an appearance on Radio 3's *Free Thinking*, host Matthew Sweet informed Wolf that she had misunderstood a crucial legal term from the Victorian era, which completely undermined the premise of her new book, *Outrages*. The revelation torpedoed both the book and Wolf's academic credibility, making her a laughing stock. And then came COVID-19.

The pandemic was hard on everybody. Billions of people were anxious, confined to their homes and cut off from their normal lives. They desperately needed a sense of community and something to do. For many, conspiracy theories offered both belonging and empowerment. Freelancers and small business owners, the groups least protected from the financial shock of lockdown, were the most susceptible. If conspiracy theories were already spreading fast, then the pandemic was the ultimate accelerant.

Ever since the Black Death, epidemics of new diseases had inspired conspiracy theories, from cholera to Spanish flu to AIDS. This is hardly surprising. New diseases are mysterious, invisible invaders that threaten our security on an intimate level and wreak havoc on society. Vaccines had also inspired paranoia, and even violence, since the eighteenth century. During the SARS pandemic of 2003, the *Washington Post*'s David J. Rothkopf coined the word *infodemic* to describe the spread of 'fear, speculation and rumor' about the disease. Like any virus, he wrote, an infodemic has symptoms, carriers, victims and cures. The COVID-19 pandemic was the first to take place in the context of the disinformation factory of social media, a flourishing anti-vaccine movement and a boom in right-wing populism. It was a perfect storm.

This infodemic was a jumble of mutually contradictory conspiracy theories. First, that the virus was a deadly bioweapon created in a military lab for the purposes of depopulation: a 'plandemic'. Second, that it was no worse than a bad cold and had been exaggerated to justify the suspension of civil liberties. And third, that it was a hoax: a 'scamdemic'. If COVID-19 was bogus in one way or another, it followed that every health measure – masks, lockdowns, vaccines – was part of the plot. While some resistance to vaccine passports could be put down to legitimate suspicion of Big Government, Big Pharma or Big Tech, much of the opposition was based on more fanciful fears. Even before the first vaccines were available, two in five Republicans agreed that the Microsoft founder and philanthropist Bill Gates was planning to use them to implant microchips in billions of people that could interact with 5G data technology.

For people like Wolf, the big villains are usually not sinister, secretive types. They are prominent liberals whose goals and methods are transparent and whose rhetoric is often blandly technocratic. Figures like Gates and George Soros make no bones about how they would like to improve the world, by promoting democracy and cooperation. But these initiatives tend to spawn nightmarish shadow versions, turning candid plans into secret plots – a Red Scare without the reds. Agenda 21 was a non-binding action plan for sustainable development, signed by 178 countries in 1992. The Great Reset was a 2020 World Economic Forum document that hastily repackaged standard talking points about the need for international collaboration to address such challenges as climate change, inequality and nuclear proliferation in light of the COVID pandemic. On the face of it, both were vague, uncontroversial and rather dull. But both were reimagined by conspiracy theorists as schemes for a genocidal one-world totalitarian government – alternative names for the New World Order. 'There is no engaging with people who think you are secretly running the world,' complained the WEF's Adrian Monck.

Naomi Wolf turned herself into one of the infodemic's superspreaders. She began publicly speculating that COVID was a biological weapon and that every measure taken against it was part of a scheme to sicken, sterilise and surveil the population. She claimed that a 'transnational group of bad actors – including the WEF, the WHO, the Bill and Melinda Gates Foundation, tech companies and the CCP – used the pandemic to crush humanity and in particular to destroy the West'. Vaccines, she said, turned people into 'ghosts' who no longer emitted odours while endangering the unvaccinated by 'shedding' viral particles – a medical impossibility.

Wherever conspiracy theorists start off, the gravitational pull is typically towards the right, which is far more adept than the left at weaponising that worldview and championing defectors from the other side as brave heretics who have seen the light. Although Wolf was initially awkward about appearing on shows hosted by furious populist conservatives like Tucker Carlson, Steve Hilton and Steve Bannon, she soon embraced her new community and cast off her opposition to Donald Trump. If your old friends think you're a crackpot and your new friends think you're a hero, then the incentives are pretty clear. She enjoyed both the dopamine hit of approval and a new income stream. As Naomi Klein wrote: 'She is getting everything she once had and lost – attention, respect, money, power.'

Conventional radicalisation requires external actors and their victims: the radicalisers and the radicalised. But conspiracy theories fuel self-radicalisation. Wolf was not the only person to lose their bearings in 2020.

Maajid Nawaz was a former Islamist who became one of the UK's leading experts on deradicalisation, founder of the government-funded think-tank Quilliam, a parliamentary candidate for the centrist Liberal Democrat Party and host of a popular mainstream LBC radio show. After the 2020 US election, though, his output became as bizarre as Wolf's: the election had been stolen, COVID-19 was a 'global fraud' orchestrated by the Chinese Communist Party, and mandatory vaccinations were the work of 'a network of fascists who seek a New World Order'. In January 2022, LBC finally sacked him. Neil Oliver, previously a popular historian and the likeable presenter of the BBC's natural history programme *Coast*, was similarly radicalised by his opposition to lockdowns and vaccines. On the right-wing channel GB News, he referenced the New World Order and alleged that vaccines caused 'turbo-cancer'. He was not sacked.

The world's most prominent conspiracy addict – the crowning example of high-speed online self-radicalisation – is also sometimes its richest man. Until 2022, Elon Musk's Twitter output largely consisted of lame jokes and nerdy promotion for his tech companies, SpaceX and Tesla. Musk was never left-wing, but he sought the approval of mainstream liberals. He made electric cars viable and desirable and seemed committed to fighting climate change. He was taken seriously when he talked about his desire to save humanity from extinction. He was compared to Marvel's scientist superhero Iron Man so often that he cameoed as himself in *Iron Man 2*.

But around the time he bought Twitter for $44bn in 2022, Musk became hooked on conspiracy theories – about COVID, immigrants, wokeness and whatever else the far-right accounts he followed were obsessed with. By 2023, he appeared to be actively promoting the Great Replacement Theory: a white nationalist hypothesis, associated with several terrorist attacks, that liberal elites are using mass migration and falling birth rates to replace white populations. (Musk denied that he endorsed the theory.)

Musk did not just give up on moderating disinformation on the platform (which he renamed X), but actively encouraged it in the name of undiluted free speech, lifting the suspensions of numerous conspiracist and far-right accounts. For a billionaire entrepreneur to become more conservative was not remarkable in itself. But Musk did so during a period when American conservatism had fully surrendered to the paranoid style, on a platform that enabled users to construct their own realities.

Countless people have undergone a process of radicalisation similar to that experienced by Musk, Oliver, Nawaz and Wolf. They start with one theory and then tumble down the rabbit hole, until they are so deep that there is no limit to what they might believe.

The conspiracy entrepreneur

'You have to understand, what you are dealing with is a thriving industry,' Dallas attorney Bill Alexander complained about the JFK business in 1993. 'People are making lucrative livings off of selling conspiracy theories to the public. What happened to the truth? Hell, it got lost under a lot of dollar signs. No one wants to hear what really happened because it would be the end of their very profitable business.'

Alexander was talking about books, speaking engagements and other mainstream activities. What he could not foresee was the financial opportunities of a democratised online infosphere with no gatekeepers. Politically committed people like to donate money to those they see as brave crusaders. They are also prone to dismissing any allegations of wrongdoing as smears. As an audience, therefore, they are both lucrative and loyal. Once they have secured this support base, conspiracy entrepreneurs often fall prey to something called 'audience capture'. They have to keep feeding the beast with a constant supply of new material, so they cannot afford to be fussy. They accumulate conspiracy theories at a dizzying rate, rarely daring to risk alienating followers by dismissing one as too far-fetched or politically toxic. The conspiracy economy thus incentivises escalation. Eventually the mask eats the face and what they actually think is true becomes irrelevant, if not unknowable. Everything is just content.

Perhaps the first conspiracy entrepreneur was the British former sports presenter David Icke. When Icke appeared on the BBC chat show *Wogan* in 1991 to announce that he was the 'Son of the Godhead' and that the world would end in 1997, he became a human punchline, inspiring gales of laughter. He continued to be funny when he claimed that the Illuminati were descended from extraterrestrial 'reptilians' called the Archons, or Anunnaki, who sacrificed children and drank their blood, and that the *Protocols of the Elders of Zion*, while essentially true, unveiled not Jews but these lizards – a superconspiracy theory. The Illuminati, he said, sowed fear and chaos so that the Archons could feed off humanity's 'negative energy'. By the end of the 1990s, however, Icke's many books had made him the world's most popular and influential conspiracy theorist.

In 2014, Icke headlined London's Wembley Arena with an eight-hour lecture called *Awaken!!* As well as the Archons, his targets ranged from austerity, bankers, Israel and GMO foods to vaccines, the Rothschilds, Bill Gates and 'the centralised fascist-communist bureaucratic dictatorship of the EU'. 'They told me 25 years ago, "You're finished. You can't go any further after all that ridicule",' he concluded with a smile. 'Watch me.'

At that point, Icke's chief competitor for the paranoia dollar was Alex Jones, a perpetually angry man with a meat-red face and a hoarse voice, presumably worn ragged by the effort of telling the truth. 'Jones is undoubtedly a new kind of talent, using cinematic imagery drawn from science fiction, informed by a deep knowledge of history, and grafting it all to a Google News feed,' remarked *New York* magazine in 2011. 'The show is a kind of poetry with an epic sweep. It's his theatrical certainty, his ability to not blink, that glues the fiction to the facts.'

As a teenager in Texas, Jones had been turned on to conspiracy theories by Gary Allen's *None Dare Call It Conspiracy* and moved on to books like *Behold a Pale Horse*. He became particularly obsessed with *Silent Weapons for Quiet Wars*, a phoney manual for psychologically controlling the population that resembles a cheap knock-off of *Report from Iron Mountain* mixed with the *Protocols of the Elders of Zion*. Jones launched his broadcasting career in 1995 with claims that Oklahoma City was a false flag and established the InfoWars website in 1999. In 2001, around the same time he was featured in Jon Ronson's *Them*, he appeared in Texan director Richard

Linklater's movie *Waking Life* as a colourful local eccentric with some entertainingly zany ideas.

Fifteen years later, however, Jones was one of the first people Donald Trump called as president-elect. Jones had supported him from the start, while pumping out conspiracy theories about Hillary Clinton. Trump, in turn, had picked up his talking points. That local eccentric had become a global powerhouse.

By then, InfoWars seemed to believe that absolutely everything was a false flag, including the Boston Marathon bombing in 2013, the massacre at a music festival on the Las Vegas Strip in 2017 and the mass shootings at Sandy Hook Elementary School in 2012 and Parkland High School in 2018. But Jones introduced a sadistic new twist to the false-flag concept. Instead of claiming that atrocities had been planned and blamed on innocent people, he now said that they hadn't really taken place at all – they were pure theatre, staged by 'crisis actors' to justify gun control. 'Why did Hitler blow up the Reichstag – to get control!' he said. 'Why do governments stage these things – to get our guns!'

As usual, a giant lie was seeded with a grain of truth: the phrase 'crisis actor' came from an acting studio that supplied students for drills and exercises. But Jones's distortion of the term was obscenely cruel. Traumatised survivors and grieving families were not just told that the worst days of their lives had never happened but defamed as paid political operatives, laying them open to abuse, harassment and death threats.

Jones was just one node in a network of 'alternative media' broadcasters and websites with common enemies: George Soros, the Rothschilds and satanic paedophile rings, of course, but also vaccines, climate science, the mainstream media and globalism. They often linked to one another and copied each other's stories to create the illusion of multiple sources – a seemingly diverse, self-sustaining ecosystem of disinformation. And they made a lot of money.

In the 2010s, Jones turned InfoWars into a $20m-a-year business by hawking dietary supplements, gold and emergency supplies for survivalists in between conspiracy theories. The angrier and more scared he could make his audience, the more products he could sell. 'Did Alex really believe it?' a former InfoWars employee said to the BBC's Marianna Spring. 'I mean, I would personally say he doesn't care whether they are crisis actors or not. What he cares about is being extremely rich, and he cares about being the king of this world he created.'

Lenny Pozner used to listen to InfoWars for amusement until his six-year-old son, Noah, was murdered at Sandy Hook and he and his partner were accused of 'profiting handsomely from the fake death of their son'. The couple fought back by suing Jones for defamation. In 2022, Jones was forced to admit to lies dating back to Oklahoma City and to accept that the Sandy Hook massacre was '100% real'. He was ordered to pay $1.44bn in damages and had to declare himself bankrupt, although he continued to broadcast. Conspiracy theories that can thrive in the wild tend to wither and die in a courtroom, a place where facts still matter.

Our third conspiracy entrepreneur is the hardest to understand because he was already rich and famous before he took that path. Russell Brand was once a successful comedian and movie star, with leading roles in *Arthur* and *Get Him to the Greek*. At the closing ceremony of the 2012 London Olympics he sang the Beatles' 'I Am the Walrus' from the roof of a psychedelic bus.

A former drug and sex addict, Brand became a politics addict in 2013 with some viral articles and interviews about the dire state of UK politics. This gave him an exciting new kind of celebrity: the witty, passionate voice of the disaffected young in the age of austerity and failed centrism. He sat down with the leaders of the Labour Party and the Green Party. In 2015, readers of *Prospect* magazine voted him the world's fourth most influential thinker.

But readers of his 2014 book *Revolution* and viewers of his YouTube channel The Trews might have noticed a conspiracist tinge to his left-wing populism. The channel's punning name ('true news') implied that this was not the false, boring news of professional journalists but the *real* news, brought to you by the voice of Dr Nefario in the *Despicable Me* movies. When the *New Statesman* asked audience members at the David Icke talk at Wembley Arena in 2014 who else they admired, Brand's name came up over and over again. As his Hollywood career faded, Brand poured his energies into podcasts and YouTube videos, where he could feed his gluttonous desire for attention.

During the pandemic, Brand's output became increasingly distant from the left-wing views he had espoused in *Revolution*. He railed against the 'terrible technocratic, globalist agenda', parroted Russian propaganda about Ukraine and allied himself with anti-vaxxers, while gently interviewing right-wing guests such as Jordan Peterson and Tucker Carlson. Indeed, the breathlessly clickbaity titles of his videos were often indistinguishable from theirs: 'Why The Left Can't Handle Donald Trump', 'Vaccine Gold Rush: Do You Trust Gates?', 'They're Eliminating FREE THOUGHT!! Billionaires' Plan To CONTROL The Internet' – the latter bearing the hashtag #GeorgeSoros. His new direction paid off. Between November 2020 and March 2022, his weekly views exploded from 500,000 to 14.5 million.

Brand's political journey was confusing to people who did not understand the nature of conspiracist politics. While it is true that his fan base shifted from left to right and he followed the money, the paranoid style occupies a special space on the map of political beliefs – a zone of smoke and mirrors where conventional ideological distinctions blur into invisibility. The binary is no longer left versus right but is instead Us versus Them. And in that world, figures who previously held opposing views on taxation or fiscal policy will suddenly find they have much more that unites than divides them.

During the 2010s, Michael Kelly's 'fusion paranoia' evolved into what *Vice* reporter Anna Merlan called the 'conspiracy singularity'. On COVID measures, for example, the far right and New Agers told the same story with different characters. For one, the enemy was socialism while for the other it was Big Pharma. Political theorists William Callison and Quinn Slobodian studied the German anti-lockdown, anti-vaccine movement Querdenker ('thinking outside of the box') and came up with the word 'diagonalism': a paranoid axis of ultra-libertarian free-speech absolutists that slices from left to right through the centre. In US politics, the embodiment of diagonalism is Robert F. Kennedy Jr. An environmentalist from a Democratic dynasty (Bobby Kennedy's son, JFK's nephew), he is also the country's leading anti-vaxxer and takes most of his support from the right. No longer particularly interested in socialism or the common good, Russell Brand is also a canny diagonalist. Like a YouTube update on Lyndon LaRouche, he attacks big business, Big Pharma and Davos technocrats but also Democrats, vaccines and wokeness. FBI director Christopher Wray christened this politically incoherent new version of extremism 'salad bar ideology': individuals can select whatever ingredients they like from the political menu.

Whether Brand is a true conspiracy theorist or just a very convincing grifter, nobody knows. Perhaps even he can't be sure. But his devoted new audience paid off in September 2023 when a joint investigation by *The Times*, the *Sunday Times* and Channel 4's *Dispatches* reported multiple allegations of sexual offences over several years, ranging from harassment to a rape. Brand denied the allegations, saying that all his relationships had been consensual, and blamed them on the efforts of 'big tech and legacy media organizations to target, patrol, choke and shut down independent media organizations, like this one'. Far from abandoning him, his fans agreed that the investigation was a cynical attempt to smear and silence him for telling the truth, as did Elon Musk and Alex Jones.

At the time, Brand had 6.6m subscribers on YouTube and 1.4m on Rumble. Talk of 'cancel culture' ignored the reality of his new career. He may have been banished from Hollywood and television, but he still had the only audience he needed.

The conspiracy leader

As we have seen, presidents from George Washington to Richard Nixon have swallowed conspiracy theories at various points, but none consumed them as gluttonously as Donald Trump. In fact, the celebrity tycoon launched his political career with one. Shortly after his appearance at the 2011 Conservative Political Action Conference, Trump began calling for President Barack Obama to release his birth certificate. 'There is something on that birth certificate that he doesn't like,' he said vaguely. He was not making a falsifiable claim, of course, he was just asking questions – the standard defensive mantra of the innuendo-peddler.

The so-called 'birther' movement (as in 'truther') maintained that Obama had really been born in Kenya, not Hawaii, and was therefore ineligible for the presidency under the Constitution. He was also probably a Muslim. The rumour originated with supporters of Hillary Clinton in June 2008 as she fought Obama for the Democratic candidacy, but it really took off the following summer, a few months into his first term, as a conservative tantrum about the first Black president. Very soon, a quarter of Americans polled said they believed it, and another 14 per cent weren't sure. The number of birthers on the right was similar to the number of truthers on the left: about four in ten. The typical birther was a white, male, conservative Republican. The spirit of Joe McCarthy, the John Birch Society and the paranoid right, kept in check for so long, was beginning to consume the party.

In April 2011, Obama bowed to pressure to release his Hawaiian long-form birth certificate. Birth announcements in two Honolulu newspapers were also dug up. But the rumours were not quashed. 'Wake Up America!' Trump tweeted the following year, sharing a link to an article on a website called Freedom Outpost: 'Israeli Science: Obama Birth Certificate is a Fake'. He then offered to give $5m to charity if Obama released his passport and college applications. When the Hawaiian health official who had approved the release of the birth certificate died from heart failure after an otherwise non-fatal plane crash, Trump implied foul play. Eventually, in September 2016, he accepted that Obama had been born in the US. But the damage had been done. In a YouGov poll the following year, 57 per cent of Trump voters said that Obama was definitely or probably born in Kenya.

The conspiracy leader uses conspiracy theories to achieve specific political goals. We have seen how Hitler and Stalin employed them to secure power and justify mass murder, and how McCarthy used them to jump-start his moribund political career. During the 2010s, Donald Trump skipped from theory to theory according to his political needs. He had a nose for the paranoia at the secret, seething heart of modern conservatism. He realised that Republicans still wanted low taxes and welfare cuts, but what really fired them up was having people to hate.

Trump could not have hoped for more of a lightning-rod rival than Hillary Clinton. After the Clintons left the White House in 2001, Hillary built her own impressive political career: first as a senator, then as Obama's secretary of state. As a household name with decades of experience in the exercise of political power, she was the clear front runner in 2016. What her supporters did not understand, but Trump did, was that she had not left behind the wild conspiracy theories that had dogged her and Bill in the 1990s. Trump supporters' shrill cries of 'Lock her up!' were not really about her contentious use of a private email server as secretary of state. They were the product of more than 20 years of claims that she was a pitiless criminal mastermind who had escaped justice. And Trump's followers believed that only he could save America from her diabolical schemes.

Once he had defeated Clinton, Trump required a new dragon to fight. This one was not a person but an idea: the deep state. The phrase originated in Turkey in the 1990s to describe a genuinely corrupt alliance between politicians, police, military and organised crime. But in the US, it was more a paranoid exaggeration of governments' standard complaints that they have been stymied by the civil service. If the politicians are not really in charge, if they are fighting enemies within, then they can say that their policy failures are not their fault, while their successes are victories against the odds. Following the leak of the Pentagon Papers in 1971, Richard Nixon ranted: 'We've checked and found that 96 per cent of the bureaucracy are against us: they're bastards who are here to screw us.' That was the emotional essence of the deep-state conspiracy theory.

For Trump, the deep state involved security, intelligence, law enforcement, the judiciary, the IRS and the entire civil service – a permanent, anti-democratic shadow government. It turned the most powerful man in the world into a courageous victim of the system and justified purging any official he thought was standing in his way. Of course, in his account, the media was complicit too. In the space of a few months, Trump changed the meaning of 'fake news' from disinformation to objectively true news that he happened to dislike. This had been the standard conspiracy theorist response to refutation through the ages: treating the counter-evidence as illegitimate on the basis of the conspiracy itself. But under Trump's authorship, it had been shortened to a two-word phrase capable of being deployed at a moment's notice, whenever reality threatened to disrupt his web of fantastical paranoia.

The first British politician to go all-in on the American deep-state conspiracy theory was Liz Truss. She was prime minister for just 49 days in 2022, in which brief time she managed to crash the economy with a catastrophic tax-cutting 'mini-budget'. Truss might have responded to her political implosion with a period of quiet self-reflection and humility. Instead, she decided that she had been cruelly thwarted by the left-wing deep state and found a sympathetic hearing among US conservatives. The US title of her 2024 book, *Ten Years to Save the West: Leading the Revolution Against Globalism, Social-ism, and the Liberal Establishment*, was the acceptable face of the paranoid style. By rewriting her abject failure into a story of a noble battle against a monstrous regiment of enemies, Truss had psychologically, politically and financially insulated herself from the consequences of her own actions.

In the US, the deep-state narrative laid the groundwork for Trump's most dangerous fantasy. After he lost the 2020 election to Joe Biden, Trump clinched the radicalisation of the Republican Party by convincing most of his voters that he had not in fact been defeated – the election had been stolen by the deep state. His claim was less a theory than an instinctive response to his rejection by the American people, but many of his supporters, including his loose-cannon lawyer Sidney Powell, expanded this petulant hunch into a full-blown conspiracy theory involving Venezuela, Cuba, China, the voting-machine company Dominion and countless US government officials. At the very same time, they were involved in a real conspiracy to overturn the result. Trump's fictions had consequences. The thousands of supporters who stormed the Capitol in Washington DC on 6 January 2021 in the name of 'Stop the Steal' had been whipped into an insurrectionary fervour by a conspiracy theory. At this stage, conspiracist thinking presented a clear and present danger to political stability in the world's most powerful country.

In 1964, Richard Hofstadter could confidently say that the paranoid style was a fringe phenomenon. Sixty years later, 63 per cent of registered Republicans inhabited an alternate reality in which Trump had won in 2020. And American democracy teetered on the brink as a result.

Russia experts found the triumph of an anti-democratic illusion unnervingly familiar.

As a former KGB officer, Vladimir Putin embodied the

history of Russian paranoia. 'The former Soviet Union is the only place where the government sponsored conspiracy theories and endlessly repeated them on a daily basis for three generations,' wrote Daniel Pipes. Remember that even before 1917, Russia was the source of the *Protocols of the Elders of Zion*. Old habits die hard.

Putin came to power in 1999, at the end of a decade of post-communist chaos. Many Russians believed that Mikhail Gorbachev and Boris Yeltsin, the men who had led the country's painful transition to liberal capitalist democracy, were secretly agents of the West who had deliberately destroyed the Soviet Union. Future Putin adviser Sergey Glazyev published an antisemitic book called *Genocide: Russia and the New World Order*. Gennady Zyuganov came second in the 1996 presidential elections by running on the claim that the Jewish-led West had been undermining Russia in one way or another for almost a thousand years. That year, 60 per cent of Russians agreed that 'the West is pursuing the goal of weakening Russia with its economic advice'.

Under Putin, Russia again became the world's leading exporter of disinformation. Russia's strategy – which has been called the 'firehose of falsehood' – is not to push one counter-narrative but to make all narratives suspect, sowing confusion and doubt. By demolishing faith in objective reality, it makes the truth a matter of choice. As the director of the propaganda station RT said: 'There is no such thing as objective reporting.' Viewers do not have to trust Russia's account. All that matters is that they distrust the Western media.

Putin repeatedly explained his invasions of Ukraine in 2014 and 2022 as consequences of his belief that Ukraine has never been a legitimate independent nation. Yet at the same time he claimed that the popular protests that ousted the pro-Russian president Viktor Yanukovych in 2014 had really been a CIA coup to install a Nazi junta that would perpetrate genocide against Russian-speaking Ukrainians. Two competing stories, aimed at different audiences. When Russian forces in Ukraine accidentally shot down Malaysia Airlines Flight 17 in 2014, Russian television advanced no fewer than four different, and contradictory, conspiracy theories. After the Putin-backed Syrian dictator Bashir al-Assad used poison gas against rebels in 2015, Russia spread rumours that the White Helmets, a volunteer rescue group, had either carried out the attacks themselves or faked video evidence of attacks that never happened. In all these cases, the use of irreconcilable narratives was a feature, not a bug.

Like his Soviet predecessors, Putin did not have to generate all his own conspiracy theories when he could adopt Western ones. Stories produced by the likes of Alex Jones were boosted by the Russian channels Sputnik and RT and disseminated online by workers at the Internet Research Agency, a 'troll farm' in St Petersburg. Putin found not just foot soldiers for Russian propaganda but active creative partners in a ballooning movement that also played a key role in the 6 January insurrection: QAnon. The most photographed man at the Capitol on 6 January was Jacob Chansley, who called himself the Q Shaman. Chansley was well known for turning up at rallies in his Viking-like regalia of fur, horns and face paint, with a placard reading: 'Q Sent Me'.

The conspiracy cult

QAnon began with a story about pizza. The leak of confidential Democratic National Convention emails hacked by Russia in October 2016 was hugely embarrassing to Hillary Clinton's campaign and a boon to Donald Trump, who told supporters that Clinton 'meets in secret with international banks to plot the destruction of US sovereignty'. But some users of the 4chan message board decided that the Trump campaign and the media had missed something explosive.

While 4chan was best known as a factory for producing goofy memes that spread to 'normies' via social media, it also housed a sub-community of misanthropic outsiders and nihilistic pranksters with too much time on their hands. In 2014, 4chan had played a major role in Gamergate, a campaign against alleged political correctness and corruption in the gaming industry that took the form of a conspiracy theory. Participants imagined non-existent connections and used them to abuse and harass female journalists.

Having combed the emails for hidden messages, the channers claimed that the frequent references to pizza denoted not a popular form of campaign-trail sustenance but a paedophilic codeword for girls. 'Hotdog' meant boy, and so on. They then attached this bizarre linguistic projection onto an existing conspiracy theory about an elite ring of child abusers. In late October, the 4chan sleuths alleged that Clinton and her campaign manager, John Podesta, were operating a child sex ring centred on the basement of a Washington DC pizza restaurant called Comet Ping Pong. This would obviously make 'pizza' a very bad codeword, but that was by the by. The Republican operative Jack Posobiec livestreamed his visit to Comet Ping Pong and improvised a catchy name for the affair: Pizzagate. The suffix *gate* had figured in the names of numerous scandals since Watergate, but Pizzagate wasn't a scandal at all. It was a complete fabrication, not least because Comet Ping Pong didn't actually have a basement.

Whether Pizzagate originated as a sincere conspiracy theory or just a prank is unclear. In 4chan's anonymised, irony-laden murk of memes and provocations it was hard to tell who was a genuine extremist and who was a bored young man amusing himself and his fellow posters by saying the most shocking things possible. Once Pizzagate went viral, though, it reached people who really did believe it. As before, media efforts to debunk it in fact introduced it to the general public, while YouTube videos about it racked up hundreds of thousands of views. The staff of Comet Ping Pong received an avalanche of death threats. On 4 December, Edgar M. Welch drove 300 miles from his home in North Carolina to 'self-investigate' Comet Ping Pong and fired his assault rifle inside the restaurant. As Welch bashfully admitted after his arrest: 'The intel on this wasn't 100 per cent.'

During Welch's trial, James Alefantis, the manager of Comet Ping Pong, who had randomly found himself at the centre of a global conspiracy theory drama, summed up the implications of the experience: 'I hope that one day, in a more truthful world, every single one of us can remember this as an aberration, a symptom of a time of sickness, when some parts of our world went mad, when news was fake and lies were seen as real and our social fabric frayed.' But it wasn't an aberration. It was just the start.

On 28 October 2017, a thread called 'The Calm Before the Storm' was posted on 4chan. It purported to be an urgent message from 'Q', an anonymous official at the highest levels of the US government. Q claimed that President Trump was about to fight back against the deep state, the Clintons, the paedophiles and so on. Very soon there would be a day of reckoning with mass arrests: 'the Storm'. Within days, QAnon had spread to YouTube, where it caught fire.

What made the 'Q drops' so addictive was their use of questions, puns and clues rather than definitive information. 'Some of us come here to drop crumbs,' Q posted in 2017, 'just crumbs.' In November 2020, Q began a drop about the election with the words: 'Shall we play a game?' It was a deliciously addictive puzzle for amateur detectives, with cool catchphrases like 'The Great Awakening' and 'Where We Go One We Go All'.

QAnon became a grand collaborative fiction about not just the deep state but a vast satanic cabal of paedophiles that included household names – a lurid new mutation of the New World Order. Most conspiracy theories identify villains, but QAnon also had heroes – led by the Messiah-like Donald Trump – and the promise of imminent violent retribution. It had more in common with Hitler's self-image as a warrior against the Jewish conspiracy than it did with theories about JFK or 9/11 – a cosmic struggle between good and evil. It is amazing that during his presidency the conspirators never attempted to assassinate the only man who could expose and defeat their satanic one-world government. Maybe they were too busy.

QAnon was built on nothing. Forensic linguists and investigative reporters confidently identified Q as 4chan moderator Paul Furber and then, when the Q drops moved to 8chan, the message board's administrator, Ron Watkins. (Both men have denied that they were Q.) After almost 5,000 'drops', Q fell silent in December 2020, shortly after Trump lost the election. Trump had arrested no senior Democrats during his four-year term. The storm never came. But none of this mattered. The game was afoot. QAnon's high-profile boosters included Republican congresswoman Marjorie Taylor Greene; the wife of conservative Supreme Court justice Clarence Thomas;

Trump's 'Stop the Steal' lawyer Sidney Powell; and General Michael Flynn, Trump's former National Security Adviser, who hailed believers as 'soldiers' in an information war. By 6 January, there was no daylight between the conspiracy theories hatched by 4chan and the ones emanating from the White House. It was one of the stupidest conspiracy theories in history, which is really saying something. But it was also one of the most successful.

In a way, even calling QAnon a conspiracy theory would be a compliment. It is not a pseudo-explanation for why there is an elite global network of child sex traffickers, because there isn't one to explain. QAnon is more like an apocalyptic cult, in which the act of belief is more important than the details of what is being believed. Like a superconspiracist Death Star, it sucked in the entire history of the paranoid style – antisemitic blood libel, the Illuminati, the communists, the Clintons, vaccines – and old books like *Report from Iron Mountain*, *Behold a Pale Horse* and *Silent Weapons for Quiet Wars*. QAnon swallowed everything and spat out nothing. This spectacular incoherence made it unusually flexible. In *The Other Pandemic*, his book about QAnon, James Ball wrote: 'Given the nebulous nature of QAnon, some people would be drawn in from wellness, some from the far right, some from anti-capitalism, and so on – letting people pick their own focus allows them to tailor the conspiracy.'

Ball spoke to people who had lost relatives to QAnon, just as they can be lost to drug addiction or religious cults. The addict cuts themselves off from all sources of challenging information, from the reality-based media to members of their own family. This process is unintentionally hastened by algorithms on Facebook or YouTube that prioritise engagement. Once they leave those platforms for alternatives like Discord and Telegram in the internet's unpoliced underground, they are truly in Mirror World.

QAnon created an entirely new demographic of political violence. The vast majority of terrorists are men, mostly under 30. But of the 79 QAnon-related terrorists identified by the US National Consortium for the Study of Terrorism and Responses to Terrorism in 2021, a quarter were women and more than half were parents. In October 2022, David DePape, a promoter of conspiracy theories about QAnon, Pizzagate, COVID-19 and the 2020 election, broke into the house of leading Democratic congresswoman Nancy Pelosi and attacked her 82-year-old husband with a hammer. Matthew Taylor Coleman, a surf-shop owner from California, was charged with killing his two small children because he believed that they had inherited 'serpent DNA' from his wife and their deaths would 'save the world'. He explained to the authorities that he had been 'enlightened by QAnon and Illuminati conspiracy theories'.

In 2022, an astonishing one in four Republicans said they believed in QAnon. This was an absurdly hyperbolic improvised conspiracy theory that had more in common with an online game than a serious hypothesis and had not produced a single accurate prediction. But faith-based narratives do not have to be literally true. They just need to feel emotionally true.

QAnon pulled together the different types described in this chapter: legions of radicalised conspiracy addicts were monetised by conspiracy entrepreneurs and exploited by conspiracy leaders. To an outsider's eyes, QAnon's beliefs are so ridiculous, so hateful, so utterly estranged from reality that its followers appear psychologically alien. But if the last few years have taught us anything, it is that the cognitive seeds of the paranoid style lurk in every human mind. Watered by certain ideas, fertilised by certain circumstances, they can quickly sprout into strangling weeds. Part of rejecting the paranoid division of humanity into Us and Them is understanding that this kind of thinking is really a matter of degree – we are all potential conspiracy theorists. The task is to understand how, and to inoculate ourselves against conspiracism.

CHAPTER SIX
The Psychology of Conspiracy Theories

Reading Richard Hofstadter's 'The Paranoid Style in American Politics' 60 years after it was written might provoke a pang of nostalgia. Conspiracy theories seemed much more containable then, more of an aberration than the norm. Hofstadter considered the paranoid style a marginal phenomenon, which only temporarily overflowed its confines – a kind of virus that sometimes infected the mainstream but was ultimately defeated by the antibodies of democracy and common sense. Clearly this is not the case.

In 2024, conspiracy theories are both more dangerous than ever and weirdly boring. Whereas they used to require some effort to piece together, they now flow from a knee-jerk denial of reality. A false flag, for example, is no longer an extreme claim but, for many people, the obvious, off-the-shelf explanation for any atrocity. Christopher Hitchens argued that conspiracy theories attempt to fill the blank spaces in official narratives, but what space is QAnon moving into except a zone of epistemological chaos, the ruins of our shared reality? The explanation lies not in politics but in psychology.

If the mental processes behind conspiracy theories were unusual, we could breathe a sigh of relief and pat ourselves on the back for not believing in lizard people or whatever out-there proposition is doing the rounds. But the reality is far more disturbing. Conspiracist thinking is not a pathology. Nor is it dictated by intelligence or levels of education. As Steve Brotherton wrote in *Suspicious Minds*: 'Conspiracy-thinking is ubiquitous, because it's a product, in part, of how all of our minds are working all the time.'

In particular, conspiracy theories play off three distinct cognitive biases: pattern perception, agency detection and proportionality bias.

Humans want to join the dots. Our minds are conditioned to find patterns in the world. And that is not a fault – it is an advantage. It is what allowed our ancestors to understand that bears were predators or that certain herbs cured particular ailments. To seek patterns was to search for cause and effect before the advent of science. Today, it is what enables us to predict the consequences of our actions and understand, for example, that walking into oncoming traffic will result in a poor outcome. If we were unable to perceive patterns, we would be dead within the space of a day.

The downside is that we are terrible at recognising randomness. If you ask an ordinary person to predict the outcome of 100 coin throws, they will fail miserably. Usually they alternate too much. They put down two, or perhaps three heads, and then think they have to throw in a tails for it to look random. But that is not how randomness works at all. The coin does not know what happened at the last flip. The chance remains 50/50 each time it happens. So in true randomness, we often get clusters of results – eight heads, say – that we would intuitively reject if trying to predict them.

Randomness is so alien to our structured minds that we typically project order onto it. This psychological phenomenon is called illusory pattern perception, or apophenia. As the Scottish philosopher David Hume wrote in 1757: 'We find human faces in the moon, armies in the clouds; and by a natural propensity, if not corrected by experience and reflection, ascribe malice and good will to everything that hurts or pleases us.'

In 2018, Dutch psychologists conducted an experiment in which they asked people a series of questions about conspiracy theories. Does the US government deliberately conceal a lot of information from the public? Did it have advance knowledge of the 9/11 attacks? Then they made up some conspiracy theories, including one that the energy drink Red Bull 'contains illegal substances that raise the desire for the product' and that the inventor of the drink 'pays 10 million euro each year to keep food controllers quiet'. This was to solicit instinctive responses that couldn't have been influenced by the subjects' friends or the internet.

The psychologists then showed the subjects a string of coin toss outcomes and asked if they thought it was random or determined. They also showed them the chaotic paintings of Jackson Pollock and asked if they saw any patterns. What they found was fascinating. Those participants who were more likely to believe in conspiracy theories were substantially more likely to find patterns in both the coin tosses and the abstract expressionist paintings. They were more susceptible to illusory pattern perception. David Lifton, the JFK researcher who mistook a Coke bottle for 'badge man', was experiencing apophenia.

Historian Rob MacDougall diagnosed conspiracy theories as 'historical apophenia' – an aversion to the role of randomness of events. A princess takes a late-night drive through the streets of Paris and ends up dead in a car crash. Nineteen terrorists wake up one September morning armed only with Stanley knives and change the course of history. 'Why did Oswald decide to murder Kennedy in the first place?' asked philosophy professor Quassim Cassam. 'And why was Oswald himself shot by Jack Ruby while in police custody? All we can really say is: shit happens. People do crazy things and there are limits to our ability to make sense of their actions. In these cases, there is no deeper meaning to be found and there are no all-powerful hidden conspirators pulling the strings.'

For a person who is extremely susceptible to illusory pattern perception, this conclusion will be intolerable. It might even be literally unthinkable. Randomness cannot be accepted. Instead, links must be found, connections established and dots joined. This dynamic is at the heart of a conspiracy theorist's thought process. The Australian academics Emma A. Jane and Chris Fleming combed through 2007's *The David Icke Guide to the Global Conspiracy (And How to End It)* and found that some version of the word *connect* appeared on 229 of its 625 pages.

Take the case of the *Ever Given*, a giant container ship that ran aground in the Suez Canal in March 2021, blocking one of the world's most important trade routes for six days. QAnon followers noted that the name of the ship's owner, Evergreen, was Hillary Clinton's Secret Service code name and the ship's call sign, H3RC, included Clinton's initials. Therefore, they concluded, the *Ever Given* must be transporting child sex slaves. It was not, of course. And in the unlikely event that Clinton *had* been using an enormous ship for nefarious purposes, she would probably not have used her initials and code name. These were just coincidences. But in the world of QAnon, there are no coincidences – hence illusory correlation.

Another example is chemtrails. This is the surprisingly

popular view that condensation trails left by aeroplanes are in fact chemical or biological agents used to mentally control the population. The musician Prince believed they were causing violence in Black communities. 'When I was a kid,' he said in 2009, 'I used to see these trails in the sky all the time . . . And the next thing you know, everybody in your neighbourhood was fighting and arguing and you didn't know why.' For Prince, making an illusory correlation between the trails and the violence was psychologically satisfying even if the world that it implied was absolutely terrifying. Apophenia is a powerful drug.

Humans are similarly suggestible to agency detection, or intentionality bias. This is the inclination to presume the purposeful intervention of a sentient agent in a given situation. Again, it is entirely normal and indeed vital to staying alive. Let's say you're walking home late one night and hear a rhythmic sound behind you. It might just be some random noise, or it could be someone's footsteps. In this scenario, it makes sense to be a little paranoid and presume the latter. If you're wrong, you might look a bit silly. But if you're right, you'll be aware of a potential threat.

But just like pattern perception, this faculty can be wrongly applied. We constantly project agency onto all manner of things that have none. In 1944, the psychologists Fritz Heider and Marianne Simmel showed participants in an experiment a short black-and-white video. It was extremely basic: just two triangles and a dot moving around a square. The participants were asked to describe what they saw. They should have replied that a variety of shapes were moving around. After all, that was all it was. There were no eyes, expressions or anything else to give the shapes the suggestion of an internal life. Instead, the participants projected all sorts of feelings and storylines onto the video: a love story, a fight, a chase, an intrusion, a defence. You can watch it online at http://trbq. org/play and see for yourself. It is almost impossible not to give these shapes agency and narrative.

This form of agency detection helps structure the illusory pattern perception that conspiracy theorists experience. It's not just that things are connected. They are connected by virtue of agents doing certain things: the Illuminati, the Jews, the elite, Them.

The first person to use the phrase *conspiracy theory* in the modern sense was Karl Popper, in 1952. Popper described what he called 'the "conspiracy theory of society". It is the view that an explanation of a social phenomenon consists in the discovery of the men or groups who are interested in the occurrence of this phenomenon (sometimes it is a hidden interest which has first to be revealed), and who have planned and conspired to bring it about.'

One alternative interpretation of events is 'institutional theory'. A conspiracy theorist, for example, would say that the media is controlled by an elite of malefactors and could be redeemed if those people were brought to justice. An institutional theorist would respond that the media is shaped by various political, financial and social incentives regardless of who is in charge.

Even that analysis can overstate the role of intention. Very often, things happen that nobody desired. As Popper put it, conspiracy theorists 'assume that we can explain practically everything in society by asking who wanted it, whereas the real task of the social sciences is to explain those things which nobody wants – such as, for example, a war, or a depression'. His emphasis on unintended consequences is antithetical to the paranoid style, in which intention is everything. This is why the John Birch Society's Gary Allen mocked it as 'accidental theory'.

The third cognitive spur to conspiracy theories is proportionality bias. This is a heuristic of the human mind that assumes major effects must have a commensurably large cause. As we have seen, this happened with world-changing events such as the French Revolution, Pearl Harbor, 9/11 and JFK. Everything leading up to those events became suddenly charged with significance. As Stephen E. Ambrose wrote: 'People are loath to believe that chance or accident can change world history . . . it is almost unbearable to accept that such a miserable human being as Lee Harvey Oswald could have killed Kennedy all by himself. There must have been more to it.' But if an assassin's bullet misses and the consequences are minor, then it inspires few conspiracy theories. A few centimetres can make all the difference.

Proportionality bias operates on the most pedestrian level. In one study, research subjects were told different stories about a computer crash that prevented a student handing in his essay. In the first story, the professor failed him, scuppering his graduation and losing him an attractive job offer. Big effect. In the second, the professor gave him an extension, allowing him to graduate in time and take the job. Small effect. They were then given two alternate causes for the events. In one, there was a widespread computer virus – big cause – and in another there was a malfunctioning computer cooling fan – small cause. Subjects who were told the story with a big effect were far more likely to think the crash had a big cause.

Now apply this assumption to COVID-19. It is hard to accept that an animal virus that spilled over to humans at a seafood market in China could cause more than seven million deaths, global lockdowns and political and economic chaos. It seems much more intuitive to think that such immense consequences must have a larger cause. But that is not how the world works. It is simply how our minds work.

These three psychological phenomena produce conspiracy theories when they collide with a fourth: confirmation bias. This is the tendency to favour information that supports your prior beliefs. Nobody who supports gun control, for example, believes that school shootings are false flags, because that conspiracy theory would serve no purpose. We instinctively take on facts and ideas that are convenient to us and do not challenge our worldview. As Fox Mulder put it: 'I want to believe.'

These mental habits are not constant. They become more or less powerful according to our emotional state. In particular, they are heightened when we find ourselves in a state of fear or uncertainty. Indeed, lack of control is one of the worst things you can inflict on a human being. If an individual can control the duration of painful shocks, they lower their arousal. If they are told the details of painful medical procedures, they typically experience reduced anxiety and can have a shorter recovery time. Lacking control activates the amygdala, indicating a fear response.

This exacerbates the psychological biases we've just been looking at. Under a state of anxiety, the mind falls back on the habits it has for assessing danger, particularly pattern perception. Parachute jumpers, for example, are more likely to perceive figures in a picture of visual noise just before a jump than they are after they have safely landed. As researchers in one experiment that reproduced this finding concluded: 'Experiencing a loss of control led participants to desire more structure and to perceive illusory patterns. The need to be and feel in control is so strong that individuals will produce a pattern from noise to return the world to a predictable state.'

This hints at why conspiracy theories become so popular in times of uncertainty and upheaval: when a political leader is assassinated, after a terror attack, amid a recession or during a pandemic. As we feel that we lose control over our surroundings, our mind works to re-establish it by projecting onto the chaos.

All of us have these mental attributes, but some of us exhibit them more intensely than others. In particular, there is a close relationship between conspiracist thinking and religious or supernatural belief.

After all, this story started with the Bible. Religious faith shares many of the same qualities as conspiracy theory. It is an attempt to create patterns out of seemingly disparate events, like floods, earthquakes and plagues. It posits that there is agency behind all these incidents, in the form of a creator, orchestrating events from on high. It suggests a cause that is as big as the consequence – far bigger, in fact – and it confirms a prior belief. It satisfies all four psychological demands. The philosopher Tim Crane summarised the religious impulse with the thought: 'This can't be all there is; there must be something more to the world.' Even the most rational and analytical people have a weakness for occasionally thinking that 'everything happens for a reason'. That is broadly the same logic as conspiracy theories about the JFK assassination or COVID-19, but in existential form.

Faith-based thinking often leads to the rejection of sci-entific evidence that contradicts the belief. For example, a 2019 Gallup poll found that 40 per cent of American adults were creationists who rejected the theory of evolution and believed that God had created humans in their present form within the last 10,000 years. The French writer Marcel Proust, who was lucky enough never to have heard of conspiracy theories, observed in 1913 that this resistance to challenging facts was psychologically fundamental: 'The facts of life do not penetrate to the sphere in which our beliefs are cherished; they did not engender those beliefs, and they are powerless to destroy them; they can inflict on them continual blows of contradiction and disproof without weakening them.'

Similar mental architecture can be found in the world of mysticism and counter-knowledge, from tarot cards, telepathy and spirit mediums to homeopathy, reiki and astrology. In each case, pattern perception and agency detection overrule analysis and empiricism. According to Brotherton, conspiracy theories are more attractive to people who believe in superstitions, urban legends, reincarnation, alternative medicine and even ghosts. This obviously does not mean that all, or even most, religious or spiritual people are conspiracy theorists. But research has shown that a higher propensity to see agency where there is no empirical evidence is a strong predictor for both supernatural and conspiracist beliefs.

In isolation, these beliefs do no harm, but the New Age and wellness communities have proved to be fertile recruiting grounds for the paranoid. David Icke, for example, came to conspiracy theories via alternative medicine, New Age philosophy and Green Party politics. Initially it felt bizarre to see hippies, DJs and yoga teachers rubbing shoulders with far-right activists and libertarians on protests against lockdowns and vaccines in 2020. But in fact a similar relationship to knowledge was shared by all the participants. Researchers in the UK and elsewhere found that individuals who strongly identified as spiritual were more sceptical about COVID-19 vaccines. This fusion has been dubbed 'conspirituality'.

Sometimes religions and conspiracy cults are hard to tell apart. The Nation of Islam is a religious sect built around the conspiracy theory that the white race was created 6,000 years ago by evil scientists. The Five-Percent Nation, an offshoot that has included members of the Wu-Tang Clan, divides humanity into three groups: the evil elites who conceal the truth (10 per cent), the ignorant masses (85 per cent) and the enlightened ones (5 per cent). It is a religion operating as a conspiracy cult. Conversely, QAnon is a seemingly secular conspiracy theory that has taken on the faith-based character of a religious cult.

Political extremists are also unusually prone to our four key cognitive biases. In fact, extremism is the inevitable destination of the politics of a life-and-death battle between Us and Them rather than one based on compromise, cooperation and consensus. If you think your opponents are traitors, satanists and paedophiles who will stop at nothing to take over the world, then all bets are off. When Lyndon LaRouche was attacked for routinely describing his opponents as Nazis and deviants, one of his followers retorted: 'Why be nice? It's a cruel world. We're in a war and the human race is up for grabs.'

The first test of the relationship between political extremism and conspiracy theories was carried out by the political scientist Ronald Inglehart in 1984. He took six European countries and looked at participants' self-placement on a scale ranging from the far left to the far right, then compared it to data on their level of trust in their nation's courts. In all but one country, he found that the further out they placed themselves on the political spectrum, the less likely they were to trust the courts. People in the centre were the most likely to trust them, creating a U-curve.

In 2015, researchers in the Netherlands and the US asked respondents to position themselves on the same left–right scale and then gave them a series of questions about their beliefs in various conspiracy theories. They also found a U-curve pattern. Extremism, lack of trust and conspiracist beliefs are tightly correlated. 'This is attributable to a style of sense making that provides a straightforward explanatory framework for the events and problems that our society faces,' they concluded.

In the UK, researchers Jamie Bartlett and Carl Miller analysed the editorial output of over 50 extremist groups, ranging from al-Qaeda to the Ku Klux Klan to the Lambs of Christ. It must have been quite the reading experience. A few extremist groups, like the Real IRA, did not engage in conspiracy theories at all. But the vast majority were deeply embroiled in them. On the face of it, the alleged conspiracies seemed distinct. Far-right groups were more likely to believe in the idea of a Jewish cabal ruling the world. Islamist groups were more likely to believe in a Judaeo-Christian-capitalist quest to destroy Islam. Far-left groups were more concerned about a conspiracy of 'international financiers' or 'global elites'. But those conspiracies all took the same basic form. 'It is striking,' Bartlett and Miller wrote, 'that there is considerable overlap and fusion between many of these conspiracies, even across groups that exist at opposite ends of the ideological spectrum.'

The researchers concluded that conspiracy theories among extremists might work as a 'radicalising multiplier', feeding back into the ideology, psychology and internal dynamics of the group. They made groups who were already extreme even more extreme, and sometimes violent. They did this through the precise mechanisms we've seen throughout this story. They encouraged the sense of an enemy that was all-powerful and entirely evil. They sealed off group members from the outside world by defining any criticism as part of the conspiracy. Crucially, they all spoke the language of Us versus Them.

But who are Us and Them? The answer to that question helps unravel the core function and appeal of conspiracy theories.

In 1994, a genocide took place in Rwanda. Over the course of a few weeks, militant Hutus murdered up to 800,000 Tutsis and moderate Hutus. Countless others were forcibly displaced or subjected to mass rapes. Exponentially more people died than perished on 9/11. And yet there are no Western conspiracy theories about the Rwanda genocide.

Why? It is not simply a question of geography. As we've seen, France quickly embraced 9/11 conspiracy theories despite the fact that the attack took place on another continent. The real explanation lies in the human conception of the group – of who Us is. Americans and Europeans might love discussing their cultural distinctions, but they see themselves as fundamentally similar. A Belgian woman can imagine herself being on the streets of New York when an attack takes place. An American man can imagine himself on the London Underground when a bomb goes off. An attack on one continent is therefore interpreted by people on the other as an attack on the broader category of Us. Rwanda was irrelevant to most people's identity in the West, so the genocide did not inspire a group reaction and the paranoia that comes with it.

This tells us something profound about conspiracy theories: they are a product of group identity.

There is a very good reason for the eternal Them of conspiracy theories. It is the necessary corollary to the purpose of the conspiracy belief itself: the supreme importance of Us. Them can be many things in different contexts: a national group, a race, refugees, the political elite, financial speculators, corporations. And Us can be as well. But in nearly every case, we find that same dynamic. Conspiracy theories are about group conflict. They reflect it. They exacerbate it. They require it.

As with pattern perception or agency detection, group identity is perfectly normal and probably a requirement of the human mind. We all feel we belong to certain groups, whether they are defined by nationality, sexuality, cultural heritage or just football. Two key qualities help explain when that normal sense of group identity will become dangerous. The first is its intensity. The more aggressively we associate with our group, the more likely we are to be unaccepting of other groups. At its worst, this becomes what psychologists call 'collective narcissism': an exaggerated belief in the superiority of one's group.

The second quality is a perception of threat, real or imagined, from the out-group. After all, not all members of different groups are the subject of conspiracy theories. The Great Replacement Theory is about non-white immigration to the West, and particularly Muslims. It is not about the rate of Japanese immigration to Europe, or how many Estonians are settling down in Canada, because these groups are not considered threats. As was the case with Catholic immigrants in the nineteenth century and communists in the twentieth, it is not so much a question of Us and Them as Us *versus*

Them. When these two requirements are met – when we aggressively associate with our in-group and feel acute anxiety about the out-group – conspiracy theories thrive. They are about identity rather than information. Like propaganda, they work their audience's group-based concerns and biases into a satisfying narrative.

There is an increasingly popular school of political thought that corresponds with these core aspects of conspiracy theories. It is populism: the belief that politics is a struggle between 'the people' and 'the elite'. Populism is a diluted form of extremism, with the same fundamental thought-patterns. On the right, 'the people' generally designates the indigenous national group while 'the elite' represents liberal politicians, civil servants, human rights lawyers and immigrants. On the left, 'the people' generally designates the working class, or perhaps 'the 99 per cent', while 'the elite' represents the super-rich, corporations and the '1 per cent'.

In each case, the worldview of the populist movement tallies almost perfectly with conspiracism. Populists have a very high sense of group identity and an intense suspicion of the out-group. It's therefore unsurprising that we find widespread and deeply held conspiracist thinking across populist movements. In polls conducted just before the Brexit referendum, 64 per cent of pro-Leave UKIP voters said they expected the vote to be rigged. Many turned up at polling stations to vote with a pen so that the security services could not rub out their pencil marks. Hungary's populist prime minister, Viktor Orbán, claimed in 2023 that the European Union 'rejects Christian heritage, carries out a replacement of its population via migration . . . and conducts an LGBTQ offensive'. As we have seen, Trump's political career has been defined by conspiracy theories, from the birther movement to 'Stop the Steal', and the Republican Party was primed to follow his lead.

The political behaviour of populists also tallies neatly with the instincts of conspiracy theorists. Ahead of the Brexit vote, Leave campaigner Michael Gove was presented with evidence from international financial institutions that departing the EU would harm the UK's economic prospects. He responded by saying that 'the people of this country have had enough of experts.' Populism's rejection of expertise corresponds to the conspiracist rejection of deep-domain knowledge in favour of sleuth work by amateur investigators. Knowledge elites are considered at best untrustworthy and at worst part of a conspiracy.

The sum effect of this assault on expertise is the ruination of the human capacity for understanding. None of us has the time to master every aspect of the world around us. We do not want to take a course in ballistics to comprehend the behaviour of the bullets that hit JFK, nor study for a PhD in virology to understand the consequences of giving our child the MMR vaccine. Instead, we trust that a system of objectively assessed qualifications entitles certain people to authority in certain areas. Without it, we can only say that all views are equivalent, that anyone's contribution to a discussion is equally valid and that the truth is a matter of opinion. We experience an epistemic breakdown – an inability to process the reality of the world.

It is tempting to look askance at religious believers and political extremists and consider ourselves immune from the seductions of conspiracy theories. That would be complacent. Those on the centre-right and left can fall victim to conspiracy mentality just like anyone else. And once they have done so, they can easily drift towards the extremes. The data on conspiracist thinking is about proclivity, not destiny. Conspiracist thinking is rooted in normal psychological processes. It can therefore become absorbed into any political agenda in order to confirm pre-existing beliefs.

The most dangerous slippage towards conspiracy theory is on the mainstream right. In 2018, Bari Weiss of the *New York Times* profiled a loose group of 'renegade' thinkers she called the Intellectual Dark Web. Six years later, the writer Cathy Young observed that most of them, including Jordan Peterson, Bret Weinstein, Joe Rogan and Maajid Nawaz, had become serial conspiracy theorists. Only two people in the article, Sam Harris and Claire Lehmann, had explicitly disavowed the paranoid style.

The paranoid right casts the entire project of progressive politics as a systemic conspiracy and reframes organic change as planned subversion. The Great Replacement Theory suggests that immigration is part of a secret plot to replace the white population with outsiders. Senator James Inhofe redefined the science of climate change as a conspiracy against capitalism – 'the greatest hoax ever perpetrated on the American people'. The organisational embrace of progressive policies, from universities to the Disney corporation, is attributed to the sinister-sounding 'institutional capture'. This alleges that, rather than adapting to the changing preferences of their consumers, they have been co-opted by an alien ideology. Mainstream conservative politicians associate long-standing progressive goals such as social justice and anti-racism with new bogeymen: wokeism, Antifa, critical race theory, cultural Marxism.

Cultural Marxism is a particularly dangerous term, which has blown into conservative discourse from the extreme right. It began with a 1992 essay by Michael Minnicino, a follower of Lyndon LaRouche, called 'New Dark Age: The Frankfurt School and "Political Correctness"'. The story goes like this. When communist revolution failed to sweep the world, Marxists decided instead to stealthily infiltrate institutions with ideas such as multiculturalism and identity politics, so that they could dismantle Christianity, the nation, the nuclear family and, ultimately, Western culture itself. The conservative writer William Lind described political correctness as 'Marxism translated from economic into cultural terms'. Cantankerous European intellectuals such as Theodor Adorno, Herbert Marcuse and Michel Foucault were retrospectively pressed into a unified master plan hell-bent on undermining the West, even though many of them were not in fact Marxists and hotly disagreed with one another.

The fiction of cultural Marxism doesn't just assign every progressive trend to the machinations of sneaky European eggheads. It echoes the antisemitic Nazi concept of cultural Bolshevism. The far-right terrorist Anders Breivik, who murdered 77 people in Norway in 2011, mentioned cultural Marxism almost 650 times in his manifesto, leading Minnicino to repudiate his essay. Yet in 2020, 29 Conservative MPs and peers signed a letter to the *Daily Telegraph* denouncing 'cultural Marxist dogma, colloquially known as the "woke agenda"'. Miriam Cates MP had no reservations about claiming that cultural Marxism was 'systematically destroying our children's souls', while Suella Braverman's controversial use of the phrase did not deter two consecutive prime ministers from making her home secretary. Conspiracy theories erode the wall that separates the worldview of elected conservatives from that of murderous extremists.

Left-wing conspiracism tends to be more grounded in

reality than the right-wing version. It starts from genuine conspiracies and cover-ups and valid observations about the mechanisms of power. For this reason, left-wing thinkers are particularly tetchy about being called conspiracy theorists. 'I'm not a conspiracy theorist,' insisted the writer Gore Vidal. 'I'm a conspiracy analyst.' The intellectual Noam Chomsky dismissed the label *conspiracy theory* as 'the intellectual equivalent of four-letter words and tantrums'. But people on the left can also suffer from faulty assumptions about the way the world works.

Conspiracist thinking on the left has a one-size-fits-all quality, making a logical leap from a correctly identified injustice to a universal explanation. A conspiracy theory may reflect a deeper truth about the abuse of power without being true in itself. As we have seen with the shocking revelations of the 1970s and 1980s, it is hard to wave away the assumption of malice: if they did this, then why not that?

When President Eisenhower coined the phrase 'the military–industrial complex' in 1961, he was criticising the collusion of politicians, the armed forces and arms manufacturers in spending excessive amounts on defence. But the phrase became attached to a belief that Eisenhower would never have endorsed – the *Report from Iron Mountain* idea that wars are deliberately engineered for power and profit. Similarly, the fact that media organisations sometimes have political and financial interests in presenting information in a certain way does not mean that the mainstream media, or 'MSM', is always lying. Nor does the documented reality of American malfeasance, from the Middle East to Latin America to Vietnam, dictate that America is responsible for all the world's troubles.

This simplistic interpretation of events might be considered soft conspiracism, but it can sometimes mutate into full-blown conspiracy theories. Left-wing critiques of global capitalism, for example, can merge with right-wing paranoia about one-world government. 'Anti-Zionist' critics of Israeli policy often use the same imagery as far-right antisemites. This hunt for scapegoats is antithetical to the aims of progressive politics, which is why conspiracy theories overwhelmingly pull people on the left towards the right rather than vice versa.

'In distilled form,' wrote Barack Obama in 2006, 'the explanations of both the right and the left have become mirror images of each other. They are stories of conspiracy, of America being hijacked by an evil cabal . . . Their purpose is not to persuade the other side but to keep their bases agitated and assured of the rightness of their respective causes.'

Even centrist liberals – the kind of people who pride themselves on being level-headed and evidence-based – are prone to developing paranoid narratives in times of crisis. The Russiagate story, which took off immediately after the 2016 election, alleged that president-elect Donald Trump was a Russian asset. Unlike the birther lie, it was not entirely groundless. Many Russian Twitter accounts had rebranded as pro-Trump accounts and several Trump operatives had ties to Russia. It was almost certainly the case that the Russians hacked the emails of the Democratic National Convention in October 2016, for which Trump publicly expressed gratitude. But like the birther theory, it seemed to offer a political shortcut that would not only explain the president's shocking victory but remove him from office. In the end, a two-year investigation by special counsel Robert Mueller could not find solid evidence of collusion that would justify the claim that the president was an actual Russian asset. In fact, the hyperbolic allegations of Russiagate served to confirm Trump's belief that the deep state and the media were out to get him. As in the Cold War's 'wilderness of mirrors', one partisan conspiracy theory nourished the other.

A similar mirroring occurred in the UK in the years after the 2016 referendum. Many Remainers explained their defeat as the result of a Russian plot to subvert British democracy via the political consultancy Cambridge Analytica. Again, there was some truth to this: many members of the establishment *did* oppose Brexit, Russian propagandists *did* want to weaken the EU, and Cambridge Analytica's methods *were* shady. The UK's intelligence committee report into Russian involvement in the referendum found the government lacked information about the operation because it had chosen not to investigate it. But lack of evidence, even if it is purposeful, is not the same as damning evidence. There is no solid foundation to claim that Russia swung the referendum.

Perhaps the most subtly pervasive example of a liberal conspiracy theory is the 'dead cat'. This refers to a tactic associated with Lynton Crosby, the Australian election strategist who worked for Boris Johnson and several other right-wing politicians. As Johnson once explained, throwing a dead cat onto the dining room table may cause alarm or disgust, but it is certainly distracting. 'Everyone will shout, "Jeez, mate, there's a dead cat on the table!"' he said. 'In other words, they will be talking about the dead cat – the thing you want them to talk about – and they will not be talking about the issue that has been causing you so much grief.'

Governments certainly do deploy the dead cat tactic, whipping up controversies to divert attention from troublesome stories. But public awareness of the tactic meant that very soon, nearly every event in UK politics was branded a dead cat: every ministerial gaffe, every scandal, every row, every controversy. Compared to most of the conspiracy theories in this book, the dead cat looks innocuous but it can still be corrosive to political debate. It creates distrust in every ministerial statement or TV news story. It helps to create the impression that the world we see around us is a charade, manipulated by malign forces. As we have seen, the single best predictor of someone believing one conspiracy theory is whether they believe another. The dead cat can therefore operate as an entry-level drug that primes the individual for further deterioration in their epistemological capacity: a homeopathic radicalisation agent.

The popularity of this relatively mild variant of paranoid thinking proves that we are all susceptible to its lure. We all share the basic mental operating processes that make conspiracy theories so seductive.

Nonetheless, there are things we can do to protect ourselves, as individuals and a society, against conspiracy theories and to restore our common reality.

EPILOGUE
How to Fight Conspiracy Theories

We know enough now to put together a more expansive definition of a conspiracy theory. It is a fictional explanation of events in which everything is connected, everything is planned and nothing is what it appears to be. It creates the illusion of coherence by attributing the world's ills to malevolent individuals rather than flawed systems or unintended consequences, on the false assumption that whoever benefits from an event must have been responsible for it. It delegitimises the authority of institutions and mainstream sources of information while valorising counter-knowledge. It therefore cannot be falsified by evidence or events. It tends to link up with other conspiracies to form a larger story about the exercise of power and the course of history that is far less plausible than orthodox narratives but far more emotionally satisfying. And it succeeds by exploiting powerful cognitive biases.

As we have seen, conspiracy theories are dangerous. In their most extreme form, they have been used to justify tyranny and genocide. They inspire mass shootings, terrorist attacks and insurrections. They encourage the harassment of reporters, healthcare workers and the victims of atrocities. They thwart the treatment of preventable diseases and action to alleviate climate change.

Even when it does not lead to such dire consequences, paranoid thinking sabotages the democratic process by eroding faith in the possibility of fair elections or objective reporting, making us more divided, alienated and apathetic. In 1995, three Stanford University psychologists interviewed people about their appetite for political activity before and after a screening of *JFK*. After seeing the movie, the subjects said they were markedly less likely to vote or join campaigns. If you believe the whole system is rigged and the secret rulers of the world prevail whoever you vote for, then why bother?

Misreading events in conspiracist terms makes the world worse because it diverts political energies into battling phantoms rather than finding solutions to real problems such as inequality or unjust wars. Conspiracy theories wreck the credibility and efficiency of any activists who fall for them. At best, they are a colossal waste of time. 'People are being asked to think about something that isn't true, so they'll be asking the wrong questions and thus getting useless answers,' the writer Alexander Cockburn complained about Stone's movie. 'This is an infantile, inactivist prescription for politics.'

Conspiracy theories also hurt the people who believe in them. We have quoted suggestions that such theories are perversely reassuring because it is better to believe that unpleasant developments are the result of a clever plan rather than accidents, misunderstandings or plain bad luck. They provide a sense of heroic purpose, villains to blame for your misfortunes and new friends in the community of fellow truth-seekers. Yet psychological studies consistently show that, on the contrary, believers are angrier, more fearful and more unhappy than non-believers. If the conspiracy is so vast and powerful that it can never be defeated, the initial thrill of uncovering it soon gives way to rage and despair. Many radicalised people cut themselves off from friends and family members, ruin their careers and reputations and even lose their lives. In April 2022, researchers estimated that one in four US COVID deaths – 250,000 people – could have been prevented with a vaccine. Fundamentally, conspiracy theories prevent people from seeing the world as it is.

For all these reasons, the rise of conspiracy theories must be halted. There is no one simple solution to the problem, no easy trick that will cure the human mind of its biases towards unreason. But we can improve the situation by adopting a broad range of approaches.

The starting point, morally as well as practically, is to separate the victims from the villains. Most conspiracy addicts aren't famous or powerful. They are confused and anxious people who have fallen for pernicious fantasies without intending to cause harm. For this reason, they require empathy rather than denunciation if they are to change their minds. The entrepreneurs and leaders who consciously lead them down the garden path for their own ends merit harsher treatment.

One thing we have learned over the past two decades is that you cannot ignore conspiracy theories and hope they go away, or at least remain in their informational ghettos. They spread, and they spread quickly. It takes just minutes to create a conspiracy theory and hours to spread it, but weeks to debunk it with primary sources, by which time it is too late. As Jonathan Swift observed as long ago as 1710: 'Falsehood flies, and the Truth comes limping after it.'

To start with the mainstream media, the first priority is to stem and reverse the normalisation of conspiracy theories. Journalists need to familiarise themselves with the theories of the day and identify them wherever they arise, even when they come from seemingly respectable political actors. But calling them out is not a simple business.

Joe McCarthy's lies were able to run rampant in the 1950s because newspapers felt obliged to cover them objectively, granting his hysterical accusations front-page privileges while relegating scrutiny to the comment pages. Balanced journalism does not mean giving equal weight to fact and fiction. During the Trump administration, some news organisations rejected this false neutrality and began framing Trump's misleading statements as lies within news reports and even headlines. But this still had the effect of publicising his lies. Several times during this story we have seen media outlets cover a conspiracy theory in order to disprove it only to end up amplifying it. It is a fiendish dilemma.

One solution, developed by the linguist George Lakoff and named by CNN's Brian Stelter, is the 'truth sandwich'. When reporting a conspiracy theory, you start with the truth that the lie is designed to obscure, then outline the lie as briefly as possible and conclude by restating the truth. The goal is to contextualise the falsehood – who is spreading it and why? – and drain its power rather than simply repeating it.

There are no hard-and-fast rules. What is required is sound editorial judgement on a case-by-case basis: when to cover the story, if at all, and how to do so. The media can also dampen the demand for conspiracy theories by providing thorough and compelling accounts of what actually took place. It was not necessary, for instance, for a newspaper to unpick every conspiracy theory about 9/11, but it was important to explain the details of what happened – the temperature at which steel buckles, say – rather than leave gaps in the story where fantasies could flourish. In moments of crisis people have valid questions, and they should be answered sooner rather than later.

When it comes to influential conspiracy theorists, lines should be drawn and taboos established. Where senior politicians engage with conspiracy theories, they should be treated like conspiracy theorists. They should be expected to understand the implications of talking about cultural Marxism, the Great Reset or the Great Replacement Theory and not get away with using that language loosely. It is unacceptable that Liz Truss is able to stand at the Cenotaph on Remembrance Sunday with all the gravitas of a former prime minister after spreading hogwash about the 'deep state'.

Only serious social and professional consequences can act as a deterrent. If someone insists on using conspiracist language, they should no longer be invited to speak at respectable think-tanks, give their opinion on unrelated matters on mainstream current affairs programmes or enjoy an easy ride on podcasts. In short, they should not enjoy the advantages of being treated as serious people. In extreme cases, sanctions are legitimate. LBC was too slow to sack Maajid Nawaz, just as the Conservative Party waited too long to suspend MP Andrew Bridgen for spreading disinformation about COVID vaccines. Free speech does not mean the right to abuse the privilege of a platform to promote destructive lies.

Mainstream sources of information are now engaged in a fierce competition with alternative sources of variable quality. The gatekeepers have fallen. We are currently witnessing the consequences of people with no digital training suddenly being plunged into a forest of dubious information, where conspiracy theories spread like wildfire on Facebook, TikTok, WhatsApp and Telegram.

Social media companies need to be quicker to suspend bad

actors, moderate misleading content and tweak algorithms to restrict the spread of disinformation. If you search for books about vaccines on Amazon, for example, the first page of results will offer you a number of shrill anti-vaxxer books. Conspiracy theories are still widely available on YouTube. The challenges of balancing social responsibility with a commitment to free speech are significant, but tech companies' hands-off approach is clearly not working.

We also need to strengthen the resistance of the consumers of media. The technology is here. It is here to stay. We must equip children with the ability to navigate it throughout their lives. Starting in primary school, they should be taught how to critically assess information in the online world. As the writer Matthew d'Ancona argued: 'Learning how to navigate the web with discernment is the most pressing cultural mission of our age.' Children should be equipped with the media literacy necessary to compare different sources of information, weigh up evidence and apply healthy scepticism.

In secondary school, educators can get to the root of the issue by teaching children about the twisted logic of conspiracy theories and the psychological biases they exploit, and then emphasise that the world is more complicated and unpredictable than conspiracy theorists make out. The antidote to the paranoid style is the acceptance of accidents, coincidences and loose ends. History is not a coherent plot but a frantic improvisation. That is not such an enticing story, but it does have the advantage of being true.

Conspiracy theories expose a society's failure to inspire trust. 'A conspiracy theory that catches on is a form of folklore,' Jesse Walker wrote in *The United States of Paranoia*. 'It says something true about the anxieties and experiences of the people who believe and repeat it, even if it says nothing true about the objects of the theory itself.'

A 2022 US Gallup poll about trust in institutions helps explain why conspiracy theories are booming. Levels of trust hit historic lows. In 1985, 56 per cent of Americans trusted the Supreme Court and 41 per cent trusted Congress. In 2022, those numbers had plummeted to 25 and 7. The media's credibility was also in freefall: just 16 per cent for newspapers and 11 per cent for TV news. Tech companies, big businesses, courts and public schools had also lost the public's confidence. Only small businesses and the military commanded levels of trust over 50 per cent.

'Trust no one' is a useful mantra if you are a character in a paranoid thriller, but it is fatal to democracy. Revelations of official deceit on an immense scale, from Watergate and Iran–Contra to COINTELPRO and the Iraq War, made conspiracy theories more popular. Asking governments to always tell the truth and reverse this trend is a tall order, but nothing fuels paranoia like the loss of trust. And with that distrust goes a feeling that ordinary people have no control over the society they live in.

As we have seen, people are more susceptible to illusory pattern perception and agency detection when they feel they have little control over events. Since the days of the French Revolution, conspiracy theories have expressed a fear of modernity, giving faces and names to anonymous institutions and forces of change. To a certain extent, feeling somewhat powerless is inevitable. We cannot end recessions or wars on our own. But we can note the acute psychological harm caused by a lack of control and incorporate it into our political system. We can think about how to help people feel – and be – more in control.

One answer is increasing civic participation and providing a variety of routes to political influence, depending on people's interests and dispositions. Some of those can be informal, for instance encouraging involvement in campaigns and protests. Some can be more structured, such as inviting the public to participate in deciding local traffic measures. Others can be high-level, like mass consultations on national policy.

In general, we would want to see laws that facilitated political demonstrations rather than criminalised them. We would want formal processes for local residents to meaning-fully contribute to the decisions made by their local councils. We might want effective public participation to be included in measures of councils' performance. We might wish to change the electoral system to a proportional one, in which each vote counts, while still maintaining the local constituency link with an MP. We could choose to deploy citizens' juries at the early Green Paper stage of legislation, so that voters can help weigh up the advantages and disadvantages of a bill before it is published. We might wish to empower the ombudsman service with pursuing public grievances.

It is not so much a question of which policy we pursue but of our direction of travel. Each time we make a decision, particularly on issues of governance, the question should be: is this empowering citizens and making them feel more in control? Or is it doing the opposite?

When loss of trust meets lack of control, it breeds a sense of furious injustice. Fostering both trust and agency requires accepting the genuine anxieties that breed conspiracy theories. Health professionals who specialise in reducing vaccine scepticism do not tell people to stop worrying and take the damn jab. They talk through the patient's concerns and answer questions as honestly as possible. During the pandemic, the media was reluctant to discuss the slim but real risks of COVID vaccines or to even consider the lab-leak theory because it was entangled with wilder claims about bio-weapons and genocide. This enabled anti-vaxxers to allege a cover-up. Dismissing people's worries and doubts too quickly can drive them into the arms of the conspiracy theorists we are trying to save them from.

So far, these initiatives require people with influence to change how they operate. If you are not a politician, journalist, educator or social media company, it can feel as if there is little you can do to restore trust and stem the tide of disinformation. But individuals can put pressure on politicians and journalists to maintain these standards. And perhaps more importantly, they can do something about the conspiracy theorists in their own lives.

Arguing with conspiracy theorists is enormously frustrating. They usually dismiss criticism as proof that they are on to something and dark forces are desperate to shut them up, dismissing the doubters as either 'highly paid' operatives for the conspirators or naïve fools. They are not deterred by failed predictions. The fact that COVID lockdowns did not result in a permanent authoritarian state, or school shootings did not lead to the confiscation of firearms, was not acknowledged as a damning refutation of their central conceit.

But just because it is difficult does not mean you shouldn't try. Many conspiracy theorists are exiles from mainstream life. When somebody is banished by their friends, family or polite society and cut off from other sources of information, their radicalisation intensifies. If you know a conspiracy theorist, the best thing you can do is keep the lines of communication open.

The most important thing to remember is empathy. Conspiracy theories have three main psychological drivers. One is epistemic – the need to impose explanations on a chaotic world. The second is threat-based – a defensive response to a perceived danger. The third is social – the pleasure of belonging to a supportive community of like-minded people. Of these, the third is the most underrated. When Facebook tried to combat disinformation by adjusting its algorithm to prioritise posts from friends rather than external sources, it inadvertently strengthened these communities of radicalisation, shutting out all other information. Talking someone out of a conspiracy theory, like deprogramming a cult member, deprives them of this solidarity. What you need to do is offer them exit routes and get around their psychological biases.

Establish common ground, however thin a strip it might be. Identify the threats and injustices that concern you both. Find out the concern that is at the heart of their conspiracy theory. What frightens or confuses them? And can you relate to some degree? Try not to be angry, disdainful or mocking. Absurd and dangerous beliefs might richly deserve a sneer, but open hostility is exactly what the conspiracy theorist expects from both those who belong to the conspiracy and those ignorant fools who do not know it exists. Even using the phrase *conspiracy theorist* triggers a defensive doubling-down. Be as respectful as you can.

Avoid head-on rebuttals. Nobody likes to be told they are wrong, especially if it involves a passionately held belief. Criticism that challenges someone's worldview can sometimes strengthen that worldview by triggering a defensive response: the so-called backfire effect. It is better to gently sow seeds of doubt and counter-arguments and ask questions about elements of the theory that don't add up.

Remember Proust's observation: 'The facts of life do not penetrate to the sphere in which our beliefs are cherished.' Conspiracy theories feed on powerful emotions and psychological biases, so you can't dismantle them with facts alone. They are compelling stories and they have to be fought with better stories.

Instead of trying to debunk the lie, focus on the truth. Use your own home-made version of the truth sandwich. Instead of challenging the content, question the source. Redirect the conspiracist mantra 'Do your own research' towards genuine, accurate research beyond their information silos. Offer facts and sources as neutrally as possible, in an effort to help them understand the truth rather than prove that they are deluded. Studies show that conspiracy theorists respond to repetition rather than new evidence, which is why echo chambers are so powerful. Puncturing their bubbles takes time.

Point out the paradoxes inherent in conspiracy theories, like the idea that conspirators are capable of pulling off fiendishly complex plots involving thousands of people while leaving so many loose threads that an average Reddit user can unravel them. Conspiracy theories promise to make the world more comprehensible, so try to demonstrate why that is an empty promise.

Make them aware of the consequences of their beliefs and actions. As the BBC's disinformation correspondent Marianna Spring discovered when she interviewed conspiracy theorists, most of them considered themselves decent and compassionate people who were doing good work. Many were shocked to realise that their false-flag theories were feeding the harassment of grieving relatives. By humanising the victims of conspiracy theories, you can appeal to empathy.

Most importantly, catch your friends and family members

before they fall too far down the rabbit hole. It is much harder to bring somebody back to reality once they have fully surrendered to a paranoid worldview. If you want to maximise the chances of any of these techniques working, look out for the signs of self-radicalisation and get in early.

We can learn valuable lessons from former conspiracy theorists. Brent Lee, who hosts the podcast *Some Dare Call It Conspiracy*, was radicalised by the Iraq War and spent 15 years immersed in the Illuminati, false flags and satanic plots, spending up to nine hours a day in online communities. 'I wasn't taught how to assess information or how to do research,' he explained. 'I don't think I lacked intelligence but I was very naïve about politics and how the world actually works.' Lee deradicalised himself after he found Alex Jones's Sandy Hook theory obscene and Pizzagate ridiculous, and devoted himself to trying to talk people like himself out of conspiracy theories by appealing to their better natures. 'Most conspiracists want a better world,' he said. 'They think something bad has happened, and they want to expose it. I think if you can lean into that with them, and say: "Yes, I understand why that would worry you, but perhaps it's not actually what's happening," I think that's a better way to approach it.'

Conspiracy theorists on the whole are not incurably strange people whose brains are wired differently to everybody else's. We are each engaged in a battle against conspiracist thinking and the traps laid by our own minds. Certain attributes will help insulate us against it: a genuinely sceptical disposition, a commitment to reason and empiricism, an understanding of how conspiracy theories work and an aversion to political extremism. But none of us are immune.

Conspiracy theories thrive on our desire for simple stories

about the world, stories that reject its complexity and randomness and instead emphasise a false sense of agency. They play on our paranoia by demanding that we stop thinking of opponents as people with different values and instead consider them an absolute evil that must be overthrown. We all have that hair-trigger itch towards simplicity and tribalism. Anyone who has fallen for a fake quote or hoax news story online will know how easy it is to believe something that suits our biases – something we wish was true. Easy explanations make us feel righteous and give us somebody awful to blame. They are enormously appealing, which is why we must always think twice before accepting them.

It is up to us to fight against these temptations, day after day, in our political lives. We must accept the complexity of the world. We must recognise that there are no easy answers. We must see that our opponents are not malevolent geniuses but people much like ourselves, with different principles and agendas. It is a thankless task, and a difficult one. But it is how we will save reason, progress and reality itself from the rabbit hole.

Acknowledgements

Our thanks to the whole team at Orion, who worked so diligently to make these books happen. They are: Lindsay Terrell, Lily McIlwain, Jo Whitford, Jane Selley and Aoife Datta, and Dan Jackson who designed the beautiful retro covers and orchestrated the design scheme across the line. Most of all, thank you to Jenny Lord, who believed in this project pretty much from the second we put out our first episode and helped carry us every step of the way. Without her, these books would not exist.

Thanks to the production team at Podmasters, who really are responsible for *Origin Story* as it stands today; they didn't just give us the equipment, they forced us to think hard about what we wanted to do and refine the idea until it became a viable editorial proposition. In particular, thank you to Andrew Harrison, Martin Bojtos, Simon Williams, Anne-Marie Luff, Jade Bailey, Jim Parrett, Mischa Welsh, Kieron Leslie, Jill Pearson and Jessica Harpin.

Most of all, thank you to our listeners. Nothing about *Origin Story* made sense when we conceived of it. It would entail countless hours of work for each episode and break away from the current affairs ecosystem, in which we had an inbuilt audience, to try something completely different. There was a danger that it would be too light-hearted for the serious-minded people and too serious for the light-hearted people. But we knew that we wanted something unusual and were delighted to find out that other people did too. Thanks to each and every one of you, but thanks especially to the Patreons, whose kind financial support makes the podcast possible – and these books as well.

Ian

Thanks to my agent, Lisa Moylett, who always has my back. Thanks to my parents, whose love and support is the pre-condition of anything I've managed to accomplish. Thanks to the London Clan of Shazia and Farrah and the Old School Gang of Souster, Swinden and Westy. Thanks most of all to Menissa, without whom nothing is possible or even worth considering. And finally thank you to Professor Tom Stafford at the University of Sheffield, who was kind enough to offer advice on the psychology chapter and to read an early bit of the manuscript to make sure we weren't saying anything too barbarous.

Dorian

Thanks to my agent, Antony Topping, for helping to bring these books to life. Thanks to Dan Jolin and Andy Eyre – we dabbled in conspiracy theories in the innocent 1990s but didn't get too deep. Thanks to Phil Tinline for his expertise. And thanks most of all to Lucy, Eleanor and Luke for their love and support when I'm down the rabbit hole of work.

Bibliography

Books

David Aaronovitch, *Voodoo Histories: How Conspiracy Theory Has Shaped Modern History* (Vintage, 2010)

Gary Allen with Larry Abraham, *None Dare Call It Conspiracy* (Concord Press, 1972)

Kurt Andersen, *Fantasyland: How America Went Haywire: A 500-Year History* (Ebury Press, 2018)

Hannah Arendt, *The Origins of Totalitarianism* (Penguin Classics, 2017) (first pub. 1951)

James Ball, *The Other Pandemic: How QAnon Contaminated the World* (Bloomsbury, 2023)

Michel Barkun, *A Culture of Conspiracy: Apocalyptic Visions in Contemporary America* (University of California Press, 2013)

Augustin Barruel, *Memoirs Illustrating the History of Jacobinism* (Hudson & Goodwin, 1799)

Jamie Bartlett and Carl Miller, *The Power of Unreason: Conspiracy Theories, Extremism and Counter-terrorism* (Demos, 2010)

Daniel Bell, ed., *The Radical Right* (Doubleday Anchor, 1964)

Steve Brotherton, *Suspicious Minds: Why We Believe Conspiracy Theories* (Bloomsbury, 2016)

Dan Brown, *The Da Vinci Code* (Doubleday, 2003)

Vincent Bugliosi, *Reclaiming History: The Assassination of President John F. Kennedy* (W. W. Norton & Company, 2007)

BIBLIOGRAPHY

William Guy Carr, *The Red Fog Over America* and *Pawns in the Game* (National Federation of Christian Laymen, 1957)

Quassim Cassam, *Conspiracy Theories* (Polity, 2019)

G. K. Chesterton, *The Man Who Was Thursday* (Atlantic, 2008) (first pub. 1908)

Norman Cohn, *Warrant for Genocide: The Myth of the Jewish World-Conspiracy and the Protocols of the Elders of Zion* (Harper & Row, 1967)

Milton William Cooper, *Behold a Pale Horse* (Light Technology, 1991)

Tim Crane, *The Meaning of Belief: Religion from an Atheist's Point of View* (Harvard University Press, 2017)

Don DeLillo, *Running Dog* (Vintage, 1989) (first pub. 1978)

Don DeLillo, *Libra* (Penguin, 1991) (first pub. 1988)

Umberto Eco, *Foucault's Pendulum*, translated by William Weaver (Vintage, 2001) (first pub. 1988)

Umberto Eco, *The Prague Cemetery*, translated by Richard Dixon (Mariner, 2011)

Richard J. Evans, *The Hitler Conspiracies: The Third Reich and the Paranoid Imagination* (Penguin, 2021)

C. F. Graumann and S. Moscovici, eds., *Changing Conceptions of Conspiracy* (Springer, 2011)

Gene Grove, *Inside the John Birch Society* (Gold Medal, 1961)

Richard Hofstadter, *The Paranoid Style in American Politics and Other Essays* (Vintage, 2008) (first pub. 1964)

David Hume, *The Natural History of Religion* (Adam & Charles Black, 1956) (first pub. 1757)

David Icke, *The Biggest Secret* (Bridge of Love, 1999)

Mark Jacobson, *Pale Horse Rider: William Cooper, the Rise of Conspiracy, and the Fall of Trust in America* (Blue Rider Press, 2018)

Emma A. Jane and Chris Fleming, *Modern Conspiracy: The*

Importance of Being Paranoid (Bloomsbury, 2014)

George Johnson, *Architects of Fear: Conspiracy Theories and Paranoia in American Politics* (Jeremy P. Tarcher, 1983)

Jonathan Kay, *Among the Truthers: A Journey Through America's Growing Conspiracist Underground* (Harper, 2011)

Naomi Klein, *Doppelganger* (Allen Lane, 2023)

Arthur Koestler, *Darkness at Noon*, translated by Daphne Hardy (Vintage, 2005) (first pub. 1940)

Christopher Lasch, *The Minimal Self: Psychic Survival in Troubled Times* (W. W. Norton & Company, 1984)

Leonard C. Lewin, *Report from Iron Mountain: On the Possibility & Desirability of Peace* (The Free Press, 1996) (first pub. 1967)

Robert Jay Lifton, *Destroying the World to Save It: Aum Shinrikyō, Apocalyptic Violence, and the New Global Terrorism* (Metropolitan Books, 1999)

General Erich Ludendorff, *Destruction of Freemasonry Through Revelation of Their Secrets*, translated by J. Elisabeth Koester (The Noontide Press, 1977) (first pub. 1927)

David C. Martin, *Wilderness of Mirrors: How the Byzantine intrigues of the secret war between the CIA and the KGB seduced and devoured key agents James Jesus Angleton and William King Harvey* (Harper & Row, 1980)

Bill McKibben, ed., *The Global Warming Reader: A Century of Writing About Climate Change* (Penguin, 2011)

Anna Merlan, *Republic of Lies: American Conspiracy Theorists and Their Surprising Rise to Power* (Arrow, 2020)

Barack Obama, *The Audacity of Hope* (Canongate, 2007)

David M. Oshinsky, *A Conspiracy So Immense: The World of Joe McCarthy* (Oxford University Press, 2005) (first pub. 1983)

George Orwell, *Animal Farm: A Fairy Story* (Penguin Classics, 2000) (first pub. 1945)

Rick Perlstein, *Before the Storm: Barry Goldwater and the Unmaking of the American Consensus* (Nation, 2009) (first pub. 2001)

Rick Perlstein, *Nixonland: The Rise of a President and the Fracturing of America* (Scribner, 2008)

Rick Perlstein, *The Invisible Bridge: The Fall of Nixon and the Rise of Reagan* (Simon & Schuster, 2015)

Tom Phillips and Jonn Elledge, *Conspiracy: A History of B*llocks Theories and How Not to Fall for Them* (Wildfire, 2022)

Daniel Pipes, *Conspiracy: How the Paranoid Style Flourishes and Where It Comes From* (The Free Press, 1997)

Karl Popper, *The Open Society and Its Enemies*, Volume II (Routledge, 1945)

Karl Popper, *Conjectures and Refutations: The Growth of Scientific Knowledge* (Basic Books, 1962)

Gerald Posner, *Case Closed: Lee Harvey Oswald and the Assassination of JFK* (Anchor, 1994)

Jan-Willem van Prooijen, *The Psychology of Conspiracy Theories* (Routledge, 2018)

Marcel Proust, *Swann's Way*, translated by C. K. Scott Moncrieff (Chatto & Windus, 1922)

L. Fletcher Prouty, *JFK: The CIA, Vietnam and the Plot to Assassinate John F. Kennedy* (Birch Lane Press, 1992)

Thomas Pynchon, *The Crying of Lot 49* (Picador, 1979) (first pub. 1966)

David Redles and Sanford Schram, *Hitler's Millennial Reich: Apocalyptic Belief and the Search for Salvation* (New York University Press, 2005)

John Robison, *Proofs of a Conspiracy Against All the Religions and Governments of Europe, Carried on in the Secret Meetings of Free Masons, Illuminati, and Reading Societies, Collected from Good Authorities* (Creech, Cadell and Davies, 1797)

Jon Ronson, *Them: Adventures with Extremists* (Picador, 2002)

Robert Shea and Robert Anton Wilson, *The Illuminatus! Trilogy* (Dell, 1984) (first pub. 1975)

Timothy Snyder, *The Road to Unfreedom: Russia, Europe, America* (The Bodley Head, 2018)

Marianna Spring, *Among the Trolls: My Journey Through Conspiracyland* (Atlantic, 2024)

Vernon Stauffer, *New England and the Bavarian Illuminati* (Cornell University Library, 1918)

Kenneth S. Stern, *A Force Upon the Plain: The American Militia Movement and the Politics of Hate* (Simon & Schuster, 1996)

Oliver Stone and Zachary Sklar, *JFK: The Book of the Film* (Applause, 1992)

Damian Thompson, *Counterknowledge: How We Surrendered to Conspiracy Theories, Quack Medicine, Bogus Science and Fake History* (Atlantic, 2008)

Phil Tinline, *Ghosts of Iron Mountain* (Head of Zeus, 2025 [forthcoming])

Jesse Walker, *The United States of Paranoia: A Conspiracy Theory* (Harper Perennial, 2014)

Nesta Webster, *Secret Societies and Subversive Movements* (Boswell, 1924)

Francis Wheen, *How Mumbo-Jumbo Conquered the World: A Short History of Modern Delusions* (Harper Perennial, 2004)

Francis Wheen, *Strange Days Indeed: The Golden Age of Paranoia* (Fourth Estate, 2010)

Gerald B. Winrod, *Adam Weishaupt: A Human Devil* (Defender, 1935)

Articles

Stephen E. Ambrose, 'Writers on the Grassy Knoll: A Readers Guide', *New York Times*, 2 February 1992

William Callison and Quinn Slobodian, 'Coronapolitics from the Reichstag to the Capitol', *Boston Review*, 12 January 2021

Chris Carter, 'I created "The X-Files". Here's Why I'm Skeptical of the New UFO Report', *New York Times*, 25 June 2021

Winston Churchill, 'Zionism versus Bolshevism: A Struggle for the Soul of the Jewish People', *Illustrated Sunday Herald*, 8 February 1920

Francis Fukuyama, 'The End of History?', *National Interest*, Summer 1989

Gabriel Gatehouse, *The Coming Storm*, Radio 4, January 2022

Amelia Gentleman, 'Escape from the rabbit hole: the conspiracy theorist who abandoned his dangerous beliefs', *The Guardian*, 4 October 2023

Joe Hagan, 'A Strange Man Is Following You', *New York* magazine, 25 March 2011

Christopher Hitchens, 'On the Imagination of Conspiracy', *London Review of Books*, November 1991

Ken Hughes, 'A Rough Guide to Richard Nixon's Conspiracy Theories', Miller Center (n.d.)

Jeffrey M. Jones, 'Confidence in US Institutions Down; Average at New Low', Gallup, 5 July 2022

Fred Kaplan, 'Killing Conspiracy', *Slate*, 14 November 2013

Michael Kelly, 'The Road to Paranoia', *New Yorker*, 19 June 1995

William S. Lind, 'The Origins of Political Correctness', *Accuracy in Academia*, 5 February 2000

Dorian Lynskey, 'Psycho lizards from Saturn: The godlike genius of David Icke!', *New Statesman*, 6 November 2014

——, 'Why comedians stopped being funny', UnHerd, 8 February 2022

Sarah Manavis, 'What is Cultural Marxism? The alt-right meme in Suella Braverman's speech in Westminster,' *New Statesman*, 22 October 2018

Andrew Marr, 'The Cloud of Unreason', *New Statesman*, 25 October 2023

Michael Minnicino, 'The New Dark Age: The Frankfurt School and "Political Correctness"', *Fidelio*, Winter 1992

George Monbiot, 'A 911 conspiracy virus is sweeping the world, but it has no basis in fact', *The Guardian*, 6 February 2007

David J. Rothkopf, 'When the Buzz Bites Back', *Washington Post*, 11 May 2003

Douglas Selvage and Christopher Nehring, 'Operation "Denver": KGB and Stasi Disinformation Regarding AIDS', Wilson Center, 22 July 2019

Jeremy Stahl, 'The Rise and Fall of the 9/11 Conspiracy Theory', *Slate*, September 2011

Jonathan Swift, 'The Art of Political Lying', *The Examiner*, 2–9 November 1710

Phil Tinline, *Conspiracies: The Secret Knowledge*, Radio 4, March 2021

Joshua Yaffa, 'Is Russian Meddling as Dangerous as We Think?', *New Yorker*, 7 September 2020

Academic journals

Kia Aarnio and Marjaana Lindeman, 'Paranormal beliefs, education, and thinking styles', *Personality and Individual*

Differences, Volume 39, Issue 7, 2005

K. Aarnio and M. Lindeman, 'Paranormal beliefs, education, and thinking styles', *Personality and Individual Differences*, Volume 39, Issue 7, 2005

H. Darwin, N. Neave and J. Holmes, 'Belief in conspiracy theories: The role of paranormal belief, paranoid ideation and schizotypy', *Personality and Individual Differences*, Volume 50, Issue 8, 2011

D. Freeman and R. P. Bentall, 'The concomitants of conspiracy concerns', *Social Psychiatry and Psychiatric Epidemiology*, Volume 52, Issue 5, 2017

R. Imhoff and M. Bruder, 'Speaking (un-)truth to power: Conspiracy mentality as a generalised political attitude', *European Journal of Personality*, Volume 28, Issue 1, 2014

J. E. Oliver and T. Wood, 'Medical conspiracy theories and health behaviors in the United States', *JAMA Internal Medicine*, Volume 174, Issue 5, 2014

M. A. Peters, (2023), 'New age spiritualism, mysticism, and far-right conspiracy', *Educational Philosophy and Theory*, Volume 55, Issue 14, 2023

J.-W. van Prooijen, K. M. Douglas and C. De Inocencio, 'Connecting the dots: Illusory pattern perception predicts belief in conspiracies and the supernatural', *European Journal of Social Psychology*, Volume 48, Issue 3, 2018

J.-W. van Prooijen, A. P. M. Krouwel and T. V. Pollet, 'Political extremism predicts belief in conspiracy theories', *Social Psychological and Personality Science*, Volume 6, Issue 5, 2015

B. T. Rutjens, N. Zarzeczna and R. van der Lee, 'Science rejection in Greece: Spirituality predicts vaccine scepticism and low faith in science in a Greek sample', *Public Understanding of Science*, Volume 13, Issue 4, 2022

B. T. Rutjens and R. van der Lee, 'Spiritual skepticism?

Heterogeneous science skepticism in the Netherlands', *Public Understanding of Science*, Volume 29, Issue 3, 2020

D. Sullivan, M. J. Landau and Z. K. Rothschild, 'An existential function of enemyship: evidence that people attribute influence to personal and political enemies to compensate for threats to control', *Journal of Personality and Social Psychology*, Volume 98, Issue 3, 2010

Jennifer A. Whitson and Adam D. Galinsky, 'Lacking control increases illusory pattern perception', *Science*, Volume 322, Issue 5898, 2008

Films

All the President's Men (dir. Alan J. Pakula), 1976

Alternative 3 (dir. Christopher Miles), 1977

Conspiracy Theory (dir. Richard Donner), 1997

Dr Strangelove or: How I Learned to Stop Worrying and Love the Bomb (dir. Stanley Kubrick), 1964

Executive Action (dir. David Miller), 1973

JFK (dir. Oliver Stone), 1991

JFK Revisited: Through the Looking Glass (dir. Oliver Stone), 2021

The Matrix (dir. the Wachowskis), 1999

The Parallax View (dir. Alan J. Pakula), 1974

Three Days of the Condor (dir. Sydney Pollack), 1975

The Truman Show (dir. Peter Weir), 1998

Utopia (created by Dennis Kelly), Channel 4, 2013–14

The X-Files (created by Chris Carter), Fox, 1993–2002

Index

INDEX

INDEX

INDEX